T0066732

The Dead Sea Scrolls: A Very Short Introduction

VERY SHORT INTRODUCTIONS are for anyone wanting a stimulating and accessible way in to a new subject. They are written by experts, and have been translated into more than 45 different languages.

The series began in 1995, and now covers a wide variety of topics in every discipline. The VSI library now contains over 500 volumes—a Very Short Introduction to everything from Psychology and Philosophy of Science to American History and Relativity—and continues to grow in every subject area.

Very Short Introductions available now:

Available soon:

For more information visit our website

www.oup.com/vsi/

Timothy H. Lim

THE DEAD SEA SCROLLS

A Very Short Introduction

SECOND EDITION

OXFORD
UNIVERSITY PRESS

UNIVERSITY PRESS

Great Clarendon Street, Oxford, OX2 6DP,
United Kingdom

Oxford University Press is a department of the University of Oxford.
It furthers the University's objective of excellence in research, scholarship,
and education by publishing worldwide. Oxford is a registered trade mark of
Oxford University Press in the UK and in certain other countries

Published in the United States of America by Oxford University Press
198 Madison Avenue, New York, NY 10016, United States of America

British Library Cataloguing in Publication Data
Data available

Library of Congress Control Number: 2016953719

ISBN 978-0-19-877952-0

Printed and bound by
CPI Group (UK) Ltd, Croydon, CR0 4YY

*For Jonathan and Alison, who make
their father proud*

Contents

The Dead Sea Scrolls

List of illustrations

The publisher and the author apologize for any errors or omissions in the above list. If contacted they will be pleased to rectify these at the earliest opportunity.

List of abbreviations

DJD	*Discoveries in the Judaean Desert*
DSD	*Dead Sea Discoveries*
EDSS	*Encyclopedia of the Dead Sea Scrolls*, ed. Lawrence H. Schiffman and James VanderKam, 2 vols (Oxford: Oxford University Press, 2000)
HTR	*Harvard Theological Review*
JBL	*Journal of Biblical Literature*
JJS	*Journal of Jewish Studies*
OHDSS	*The Oxford Handbook of the Dead Sea Scrolls*, ed. Timothy H. Lim and John J. Collins (Oxford: Oxford University Press, 2010)
RevQ	*Revue de Qumrân*
SAIP	*On Scrolls, Artefacts and Intellectual Property*, ed. Timothy H. Lim, Hector L. MacQueen, and Calum Carmichael (Sheffield: Sheffield Academic Press, 2001)

Chapter 1
The Dead Sea Scrolls as cultural icon

The year 2017 marks the seventieth anniversary of the discovery of the Dead Sea Scrolls. Many people have heard of the Dead Sea Scrolls, but few know what they are or the significance they have for our understanding of the Old Testament or Hebrew Bible, ancient Judaism, and the origins of Christianity. Since their discovery in 1947, and especially from 1991 when all the remaining unedited scrolls were released to the world at large, there has been a surge of publications, ranging from the popular to the technical. The technical works are inaccessible to most people apart from specialists, and the popular print copies and ebooks vary in quality, from the sensational blockbusters (often involving a Vatican conspiracy theory) to the sound and reliable.

In this Very Short Introduction to the Dead Sea Scrolls, I will discuss the discovery, the controversies and personalities involved in the scholarly debates, the legal actions, the politics, and the vested religious interests. Moreover, I will introduce traditional and specialist studies of Jewish history and thought between 200 BCE and 70 CE, the archaeology of the Khirbet Qumran (the area where the scrolls were discovered), palaeography ('study of old handwriting'), textual criticism, philology, linguistics, and ancient biblical exegeses. There will also be a discussion of the most recent technological advances, often neglected by introductory textbooks. In keeping with the aims of this series, the treatment of each topic will necessarily be brief and selective; the intention is to whet your appetite and to pique your interest rather than to provide a comprehensive introduction to the Dead Sea Scrolls.

A newspaper headline in *The Independent* on 12 November 2004 read 'Afghanistan wants its "Dead Sea Scrolls of Buddhism" back from UK'. The article, written by Nick Meo, reported that Dr Sahyeed Rahneen, the Minister for Culture and Information of Afghanistan, was attempting to restore the collection of the Kabul Museum and would be formally requesting the return of the Kharosti scrolls from the British government. The Kabul Museum had been ransacked during the war that ousted the Taliban government and the collection of sixty fragments of scrolls, written on birch bark and in the ancient script of Kharosti, disappeared into the antiquities market before resurfacing at the British Library in 1994.

On 26 July 2006, the BBC covered a story of the discovery of a book of Psalms in Latin in a bog at Faddan More in North Tipperary with the headline 'Irish Dead Sea Scrolls in bog'. This 8th-century Irish Psalter was serendipitously found by the driver of a digger extracting peat with a mechanical hoe and originally contained all 150 psalms of the traditional book of Psalms. It is written on sixty pages of vellum and hailed as the most spectacular find of manuscripts of the Middle Ages for several centuries. The book was restored and in May 2014 was put on display at the National Museum of Ireland. IrishCentral.com reported that Dr Patrick Wallace, the museum director, described the accidental find of the book to be 'more important for Ireland than the discovery of the Dead Sea Scrolls'.

Notable is the way the newspaper headlines, journalists, directors, and curators of museums and libraries used 'the Dead Sea Scrolls' to signify a collection of ancient manuscript finds. The Kharosti texts are Buddhist scrolls dating to the 1st century CE and have no historical connection to Judaism. They are significant for the study of the early development of Buddhism and the search for the historical Buddha. The comparison, suggested by the staff of the British Library, was intended to underscore their great antiquity and importance. The Faddan More Psalter may be a book of Psalms, but it attests to early Christian tradition and book production in Ireland rather than the transmission of the biblical text in early Judaism. The peculiar usage of the name is evidence that the Dead Sea Scrolls have taken on a symbolic status. They are no longer just the scrolls of a Jewish sect that lived by the Dead Sea, but represent any important discovery of ancient manuscripts.

In transcending, so to speak, the historical context of Second Temple Judaism (515 BCE–70 CE), the Dead Sea Scrolls have become a cultural icon. Popular fiction, such as the bestseller *The Da Vinci Code* by Dan Brown, includes references to them in order to add intrigue and mystery to the story. Or again, in an earlier novel called *The Mandelbaum Gate*, published in 1965 by Muriel Spark, the well-known author of *The Prime of Miss Jean Brodie*, the fiancé of the main character works as an archaeologist excavating Khirbet Qumran. How did the scrolls become so popular?

The media and the scrolls

The reasons for the popularity of the Dead Sea Scrolls are not difficult to discern. From their initial discovery by two Bedouin shepherds in 1947 to the 'battle for the scrolls' in the late 1980s and early 1990s, the media have always been involved in reporting the finds, the politics, the personalities, and the academic squabbles to an interested public. Some of the reporting trades on sensationalism, with or without the backing of one or more academics; other reports offer sound coverage of the latest developments in scrolls research; and there is, moreover, a whole range of other types of publicity between these poles. In any case, the involvement of the media—newspapers, television, and radio—have ensured that the public, especially in the United

Kingdom, United States, Canada, and Australia, would have read or heard about the Dead Sea Scrolls.

One of the events that garnered considerable press coverage was the so-called 'battle for the scrolls'. Essentially, the conflict was drawn between a small group of scholars who had in their possession unpublished material from the largest depository of the eleven caves of Qumran, Cave 4, and others who wanted and demanded access to them for research and study. The tension between the haves and have-nots had been building up for several years, but it came to a head in the summer and autumn of 1991. On 29 October 1991, after much bad blood had been spilt, the battle was won by the advocates of free access when it was announced by the Israel Antiquities Authority that a new policy of access was being implemented. An article reported in *The Times* heralded the news with this headline: 'Israel opens access to the Dead Sea scrolls'.

Within weeks of the announcement of the new policy, two American scholars, Michael Wise, then of the University of Chicago, and Robert Eisenman, formerly of California State University at Long Beach, announced to the world the discovery among the hitherto unpublished scrolls of a small fragment that allegedly attests to a slain or pierced messiah. A seminar in Oxford was organized that examined the six-line text, concluding that quite to the contrary the fragment does not speak of a messiah who is slain but rather an anointed Prince of the Congregation who puts his enemy to death. These diverging interpretations will be discussed in Chapter 11 on the relationship between the scrolls and early Christianity.

The seminar was covered by a journalist, Oliver Gillie, and his article appeared on the front and inside page of *The Independent* published on 27 December 1991. One of the features of the seminar that was highlighted in the subsequent reporting was the use of computer technology and imaging software to enhance the Hebrew script. The imaging equipment was available at Yarnton of the Oxford Centre for Hebrew and Jewish Studies as part of the Qumran Project, funded by an anonymous donor and under the guidance of Alan Crown, formerly of the University of Sydney. I had produced an enlarged and enhanced image of what turned out to be fragment 5 (now renumbered as 7) of 4Q285 (4 = Cave 4; Q = Qumran; and 285 = the number assigned to the scroll), which was subsequently published in the *Journal of Jewish Studies*. This was one of the first applications of imaging software to the study of the scrolls.

Several aspects of the battle for the scrolls are noteworthy. First, the date of the publication of the newspaper article coincided with the Christmas season. This was reasonable since the Oxford seminar was convened on 20 December. Over the years, however, I have noticed that the pattern of media reports and broadcasts, in the broadsheets, on the radio, or television, almost always follows Christmas or Easter. Of course, this should not be surprising, since the scrolls are religious documents and are of particular interest during the annual cycle of festivals, but it is the Christian, and not Jewish, holy days that are followed. The fact that the movable feast of Easter is based upon the date of the Passover does not detract from the point that the media have in their sights the Christian rather than Jewish religious cycle. Why not publish reports to correspond to the Jewish New Year or Yom Kippur (Day of Atonement), for instance, since almost all scholars believe that the scrolls are Jewish and not Christian?

The reason is that it is the connection to Christianity that makes the scrolls sensational. If, for instance, 'a slain messiah' could be found in one of the Dead Sea Scrolls, then some have argued that it would call into question the uniqueness of Jesus and the foundations of the Christian faith. As an aside, this type of argument, baldly stated as it often is in the media, depends upon a rather simplistic understanding of Jesus and the Christian faith in supposing that the discovery of an archaeological artefact would undermine Christianity in this way. Within Jewish history, Jesus was not the only person to have been considered a messiah, even a suffering one, by his followers. Regardless, it could be argued that 'a slain messiah' figure in the scrolls would not question the uniqueness of Christ, but would rather underscore the view increasingly accepted by Christians in the post-Holocaust, interfaith dialogue that Jesus was a Jew and not a Christian.

Second, the application of modern technology to the study of ancient manuscripts has its own inherent fascination, the contrast between the very old manuscripts and cutting edge electronic tools. With the explosion of computer applications and web technology, there are now impressive internet sites. For instance, the Orion Center for the Study of the Dead Sea Scrolls and Associated Literature (<http://orion.mscc.huji.ac.il/>) of the Hebrew University of Jerusalem, will allow a 'surfer' to take a virtual visit of Khirbet Qumran, join an ongoing discussion group, and search the bibliographical database.

Computer technology is used in an increasing number of applications for scrolls research and the dissemination of information. In 1997, I edited 'The Dead Sea Scrolls Electronic Reference Library', a CD-ROM database that would allow scholars to search for images of specific scrolls, enhance, and print them out for personal study. This was followed by volume 2, produced by the Foundation for Ancient Research and Mormon Studies, Brigham Young University, with a database edited by Emanuel Tov, including a searchable transcription and translation of all the non-biblical scrolls. Today, several of the electronic Bible study tools include one or more modules of the Dead Sea Scrolls.

Other notable developments and projects in the United States include the enhancing and reduction of background 'noise' of a text called *Genesis Apocryphon* by Gregory H. Bearman, a scientist of the Jet Propulsion Laboratory in Pasadena, who specializes in analysing satellite images. Bearman developed a technique called multi-spectral imaging to produce readings (for instance, 'the book of Noah') invisible to the human eye from the badly deteriorated script.

The Dead Sea Scrolls are now accessible on the internet, produced with advanced digital technology. Google and the Israel Museum in Jerusalem have mounted on their website digitized images of five of the best preserved scrolls: the Great Isaiah Scroll, the War Scroll, the Commentary on the Habakkuk Scroll, the Temple Scroll, and the Community Rule Scroll. These images are so good that scholars find them suitable for use in research (<http://dss. collections.imj.org.il>). There is a scrolling- and zoom-function for each image, numbered according to column. Additionally, the Great Isaiah Scroll has an accompanying English translation that pops up when the cursor is hovering over a verse and the image can be digitally manipulated to look like an actual scroll being rolled and unrolled. The other scrolls and fragments are being digitized and made available at the Leon Levy Dead Sea Scrolls Digital Library by the Israel Antiquities Authority (<http://www. deadseascrolls.org.il/?locale=en_US>).

Access to the Cave 4 scrolls and the reading of a putative 'slain messiah' fragment are two of the controversies. There have been others in the eventful past seventy years. For instance, John Allegro, a British scholar at the University of Manchester, led expeditions to the Judaean Desert to hunt for the treasures mentioned in the Copper Scroll.

This scroll from Cave 3 is unique among the Dead Sea Scrolls in using copper as its writing material. All the other scrolls were written on skin or papyrus. The text, etched on copper plates, describes sixty-four hiding places of gold, silver, temple sacrifices, and another copy of the same scroll in the Judaean Desert. These treasures are what Allegro set out to find. Other scholars interpret the treasures, amounting to some 65 tons of silver and 25 tons of gold, as literary fiction and liken the copper scroll to the text *massekhet kelim* ('tractate of the temple vessels'), a medieval text that described how the treasures of the Solomonic Temple were sequestered to a tower in Baghdad and their hiding places recorded on a copper tablet. Allegro failed to turn up any treasure, but his expeditions were widely reported in the media.

Tourism and the Dead Sea Scrolls

Another reason for the popularity of the Dead Sea Scrolls is tourism. Every year thousands of tourists and pilgrims descend on Israel, visiting places holy to Judaism, Christianity, and Islam. Among them the archaeological site of Khirbet Qumran in the Judaean Desert and the Shrine of the Book of the Israel Museum figure high on the list of places to visit. At Khirbet Qumran they are led by informed guides around the archaeological site and are given a viewing of the nearby caves. The number of tourists who visit each year is impressive. Interested consumers can purchase facsimiles of scrolls and the jars in which some of the manuscripts were stored, as well as a whole range of souvenirs, including 'Dead Sea Scrolls' pens, t-shirts, ties, scarves, and mud. For those who prefer their visit at the click of the button, there is now a virtual, three-dimensional, immersive virtual tour of the archaeological site (<http://www.3disrael.com/dead_sea/qumran.cfm>). Social media host numerous pages devoted to the Dead Sea Scrolls where the public would be able to follow the latest developments in research.

Politics and the Dead Sea Scrolls

The Dead Sea Scrolls are regarded as a cultural icon in Israel. On 20–25 July 1997, scholars from around the world were invited to Jerusalem to mark the Jubilee celebration of the discovery of the Dead Sea Scrolls. Among the many events of this occasion was the memorable opening of the proceedings by the then prime minister of Israel, Benjamin Netanyahu; the former mayors of Jerusalem, Teddy Kolleck and Ehud Olmert; and James Snyder, the director of the Israel Museum. Sitting outdoors on the grounds of the Israel Museum and in the dimming light of a Jerusalem evening, I along with Christian, Jewish, and other scholars from Israel and abroad heard of how the scrolls were politically significant to the State of Israel. The year of the discovery of the scrolls, 1947, coincided with the re-establishment of the Jewish State after some 2,000 years. The scrolls, we were told, played a symbolic role in the return of the Jewish people to their origins, and this point was underscored by the setting of the ceremony. It was a marvellous celebration and there was even a specially commissioned musical composition by Michael Wolpe whose libretto is based upon texts from the scrolls. The Shrine of the Book, a specially constructed underground museum built to display the Dead Sea Scrolls, has an above ground structure that was built to resemble the lid of an ancient jar in which some of the scrolls were kept. We were seated in front of it and in the background was Israel's parliament, the Knesset (see Figure 1).

The political capital made out of the Dead Sea Scrolls by Israel's leading politicians was not lost on us, but a dignified silence was

1. The Shrine of the Book, Israel Museum.

maintained. It was only when it was mentioned that the Dead Sea Scrolls were vital for Jerusalem did a disapproving titter ripple through the audience. This was amusing to those assembled, since most experts believe that the Dead Sea Scrolls belong to a pious Jewish group of Essenes who, among other things, held that the Jerusalem priesthood was corrupt and as a result separated themselves from the majority of the people and went into a self-imposed exile in the Judaean Desert!

When the scrolls were first discovered in 1947, Khirbet Qumran, the caves associated with it, and the Judaean Desert were under the authority of the British Mandate and the Antiquities Ordinance of 1929. With the political changes after 1948, almost all of the scrolls fell into Israeli hands. Most are kept at the Shrine of the Book and the Rockefeller Museum in East Jerusalem. The Copper Scroll is an exception and still finds its home in the Department of Antiquities in Amman, Jordan. There are also a few fragments in the Bibliothèque nationale de Paris and scattered in private collections throughout the world. There is even one stamp-size fragment, the so-called 'McGill fragment', in Canada. Ownership of antiquities, in general, is a much disputed issue that carries a complex set of political and legal considerations. Using the legal principles of succession and territorial link Wojciech Kowalski has argued that 'the fact that the scrolls are currently stored in Israel is in full harmony with international standards of the protection of cultural property'. Not everyone will agree with this view. Legal considerations of ownership aside, there is little doubt that the scrolls belong first and foremost to the Jewish people before they are humankind's common heritage.

In the United Kingdom, the political association was explicit in the 1998 'Scrolls from the Dead Sea' exhibition at the Kelvingrove Art Gallery and Museum in Glasgow. The Israel Antiquities Authority had decided to allow an exhibit of the Dead Sea Scrolls to be set up in Glasgow as recognition of the Jewish community there and in celebration of the fiftieth anniversary of the founding of the State of Israel. The Jubilee exhibition was the only one to be held in Britain and it attracted hundreds of thousands of people.

The Vatican and the Dead Sea Scrolls

A conspiracy theory involving the Vatican has long been attached to the publication of the scrolls. It is unclear who originally came up with the conspiracy theory, but John Allegro was certainly one of the first to have expressed it. According to him, the original team of international, inter-denominational scholars had access to all the scrolls and the publication of the manuscripts was progressing apace in the early 1950s. By the late 1950s, however, John Allegro was beginning to suspect a Catholic monopoly and even conspiracy. Certain members of the editorial team were being assigned more and more of the manuscripts; Josef Milik, Jean Starcky, and John Strugnell, all Catholics, were given the lion's share. Allegro had remarked to a friend: 'I am convinced that if something does turn up which affects the Roman Catholic dogma, the world will never see it'. This suspicion has two notable features. First was his exclusion from access to the remaining unpublished scrolls. Even though he was one of the original editors, by the late 1950s, Allegro felt debarred from the team. In a letter he wrote to Frank Cross, another original editorial team member, on 5 August 1956, Allegro stated that 'the non-Catholic members of the team are being removed as quickly as possible'. The second feature was that a suspicion was being cast that the Vatican might repress information damaging to the Christian faith.

Allegro's account of the delay in publication of the Dead Sea Scrolls and the restriction of access to the remaining unpublished material have been recounted by his daughter Judith Anne Brown in *John Marco Allegro: Maverick of the Dead Sea Scrolls*. Using private letters and personal recollections, she described how Allegro attributed his exclusion from the team of editors to a

Catholic monopoly and conspiracy of silence, although she could not find any evidence to support her father's suspicions.

John Strugnell, a former editor-in-chief of the official publication series *Discoveries in the Judaean Desert*, and Geza Vermes, one of the most vocal critics of the original editorial team, have given different accounts of the publication process and restriction of access. Strugnell and Vermes were on opposite sides of 'the battle for the scrolls', but neither scholar attributed the delay and access issues to a Vatican conspiracy. Strugnell defended the speed of publication of the scrolls as comparable to other projects of the kind, like the editing of the Oxyrhynchus papyri from Egypt, whereas Vermes blamed Roland de Vaux, excavator of Khirbet Qumran and the first editor-in-chief of the 'Discoveries in the Judaean Desert' publication project, in appointing a team too small to cope with the demanding task of editing thousands of fragments.

John Allegro's view of a Catholic conspiracy is dubious, since at least one of the original team members, Frank Moore Cross, Professor Emeritus at Harvard University, who remained on the editorial team, is not Catholic. There are more mundane reasons, including academic aspirations and jealousies, personal problems and conflicts, financial constraints, perfectionism, procrastination, and the fragmentary state of preservation of the remaining unpublished scrolls that can account for both the delay and restriction of access.

In any case, the Vatican conspiracy theory continued to circulate in the public arena. Fact and fiction often became blurred. Consider the novel *The Judas Testament* (1994) by Daniel Easterman, which vividly describes an imagined conspiracy to suppress information damaging to Christian faith. The hero, a certain Jack Gould, a doctoral candidate working on the prophecies of the star and sceptre in the Damascus Document at Trinity College Dublin, is hot on the trail of the Jesus Papyrus which apparently came from one of the caves by Qumran. While Gould is following clues elsewhere, in the Old City of Jerusalem in the fictitious Catholic Institute for Biblical Studies, a certain Father Raymond Benveniste struggles with his conscience as he contemplates the fate of an Aramaic fragment in his possession. I cite extracts from it to give you a flavour of one imagined version of the conspiracy theory.

> Father Raymond Benveniste took a handkerchief from his pocket, coughed into it, and replaced it.... On the desk in front of him lay a papyrus fragment sixteen centimetres by twenty-one. It contained thirty lines of Aramaic writing, marred here and there by holes or smudges, but generally legible.... It was not much importance in itself. Just a letter to a Temple functionary from an unknown correspondent.... Ordinarily, Benveniste would have passed it on for further study and eventual publication in an issue of the Institute's quarterly journal. But for one thing.
>
> The fragment contained a reference, admittedly brief, to 'the followers of Jesus', a group seemingly attached to the Temple in some way and 'zealous for the Law of Moses'. There were, of course, several possible interpretations of the passage. On its own, it would send out few ripples....
>
> But there were people in Rome who preferred caution above all things. On his last visit, Della Gherardesca of the Biblical Commission had spoken frankly with him. A number of books had been published recently, suggesting that Jesus Christ had been little more than a Hasid, a Jewish holy man, and that his father had been a scholar, a naggar—the Aramaic word for 'carpenter' used metaphorically....
>
> Benveniste looked at the scrap of papyrus again. It was hardly important. But it could be considered yet another piece of confirmation for such scandalous theories. In the wrong hands it could be put to wicked use.
>
> He took a box of matches from his pocket. As a scholar, he was ashamed of what he was about to do. As a priest he had been trained in obedience. His hand did not even shake as he struck the match.

The Judas Testament is a tale involving an obedient priest's destruction of an Aramaic fragment that evidently attested to Jesus's zeal for the Mosaic law. The conspiracy centres on the suppression of information, accidentally found and not transmitted through official Christian channels, which would represent Jesus in a different light from the way he is depicted in the Gospels. In this novel, the papyrus shows that contrary to the way that he is portrayed in the New Testament, Jesus did not abrogate *halakha* or Jewish law. He was a pious man and a zealot of the law. The story is entirely fictional, but Easterman's Jesus has similarities to Geza Vermes's well-known argument, published in *Jesus the Jew* (1973), that the man from Nazareth is best seen as a *hasid*. The difference is that Vermes's Jesus was a charismatic holy man, not an expert of Jewish law. Even Easterman's use of the metaphorical understanding of the Aramaic word *naggar*, not as its literal meaning of 'carpenter' but 'scholar', is based on Vermes's work, although the latter has since retracted the view.

The Dead Sea Scrolls Deception by Michael Baigent and Richard Leigh, published a few years earlier in 1991, however, was not fiction. It claimed to have uncovered the sensational story behind the religious scandal of the century. The blame for the publication delay was laid at the threshold of the Vatican that was supposedly in control of de Vaux, who was also director of the Dominican centre of the biblical and archaeological school in Jerusalem, L'Ecole biblique et archéologique française de Jérusalem. It was alleged that there was a conspiracy, in the form of a modern inquisition by the Pontifical Biblical Commission and the Congregation for the Doctrine of the Faith, led by Cardinal Joseph Ratzinger (Pope Benedict XVI), to suppress unpublished Qumran scrolls that might be 'inimical to Church doctrine'.

Conspiracy theories, by their nature, depend upon some known material that has been inexplicably concealed. The lack of access to the Dead Sea Scrolls by some scholars seemed ideal as the subject of a conspiracy theory. When *The Dead Sea Scrolls Deception* appeared, however, it did not have the impact in the United Kingdom that might have been hoped for. This was primarily due to the announcement, a few months after its publication, of the new policy of access. The theory of a Vatican concealment could now be tested, and it was evident to most scholars that 'the smoking gun', to use a recent analogy, was not to be found. Subsequent interviews with the authors that were published in the media, suggested that the Vatican would already have destroyed anything that was doctrinally damaging. For most Britons, this smacked of special pleading.

When the book was translated into German as *Die Verschlusssache Jesus: Die Qumranrollen und die Wahrheit über das frühe Christentum* ('The Secret File of Jesus: The Qumran Scrolls and the Truth about Early Christianity') and its chapters serialized in a national magazine, *Der Spiegel*, it became a bestseller. In fact, the book was so popular, with sales of over 300,000 copies, that German academics felt compelled to write refutations of it.

The Biblical Archaeology Society and the Dead Sea Scrolls

For the lay readership, one magazine stands out in popularizing the scrolls and that is *Biblical Archaeology Review* of the Biblical Archaeology Society, Washington, DC. This monthly magazine, founded and edited by Hershel Shanks, the indefatigable lawyer-turned-publisher, is known for the high quality of its articles. *BAR*, as it is known by over 300,000 readers of the magazine, is often controversial as it publishes the latest finds related to biblical archaeology and the Dead Sea Scrolls. Through its publications and public seminars, the Biblical Archaeology Society has played an important role in the dissemination of knowledge about the scrolls. It also championed 'the liberation of the scrolls'.

Copyright, intellectual property, and the Dead Sea Scrolls

The battle over access to the Cave 4 material in the early 1990s included at least two legal and academic collateral skirmishes about the propriety of transcriptions and translations of then unpublished Dead Sea Scrolls. The more notorious of these was the clash over the unauthorized publication of a transcription of a text called '4QMMT' (MMT stand for the Hebrew *miqsat ma'aseh ha-torah* or 'some precepts of the torah'). In an attempt to free the remaining scrolls from the academic control of a small group of scholars, in 1991 the Biblical Archaeology Society published a two-volume set of photographs entitled 'A Facsimile of the Dead Sea Scrolls. Prepared with an Introduction and Index' by Robert H. Eisenman and James M. Robinson. At the head of the volume was a foreword, written by Hershel Shanks, which included the transcription of a working copy of the composite text of MMT.

MMT is a text between 116 and 135 lines (the number of lines changed in the course of the editing process) that discusses some twenty or so legal points of dispute between unknown individuals and groups identified simply as 'you' (in the singular and plural), 'we', and 'they'. It is believed that this text refers to an early stage of the Qumran community's split from the majority of the Jewish people. The composite text was the editorial reconstruction of the presumed original text from six copies of the scroll. The editorial process was a collaborative effort between Elisha Qimron and John Strugnell. Hartmut Stegemann, a professor from Göttingen University well-known for his methods of reconstructing scrolls, also publicly stated in a conference in Basel on 7 August 2001 that he had a hand in the editorial process, but he did not stake a claim in the legal proceedings. Qimron, but not Strugnell, sued the Biblical Archaeology Society, its president, Hershel Shanks, and the two editors, Eisenman and Robinson, for copyright infringement. The case was tried in Israel and on 30 March 1993, the District Court of Jerusalem, with the then judge, Dalia Dorner, found in favour of the plaintiff. An appeal was lodged and the Supreme Court of Israel, sitting as the Appellate Court for Civil Appeals, upheld the decision of the Jerusalem court on 17 March 1998.

The case has had far reaching ramifications for the legal definition of an author, because editorial work, in the form of reconstruction and transcription, of a 2,000-year-old manuscript written by someone else can now be legally protected under copyright law. Copyright of the composite text of MMT belongs to Elisha Qimron. The case was a watershed in copyright law and *Houston Law Review* 38.1 (2001) devoted a whole issue to a book-length discussion of the case by David Nimmer, a leading American copyright lawyer, who questioned the original judgment and subsequent appeal decision. Hector MacQueen, former professor of law at the University of Edinburgh and current Scottish law commissioner, takes a different view and agrees with the judgment of the Jerusalem District Court, suggesting that editorial work should be protected by copyright law. At issue is the criterion of 'originality' in the legal definition of authorship. Broadly speaking, American copyright law sets the bar of originality very high, requiring as it does, 'sparks of creativity', whereas the Israeli and British ones confer originality on 'the right kind of skill and labour'.

MacQueen further argues that conferring copyright on edited texts will positively promote rather than hinder scholarship: potential editors will have an incentive to expend the labour with the reward of copyright protection; and publishers will maintain their economic interest to publish edited texts. Whatever view one takes on the case of *Qimron v. Shanks et al.*, a precedent has been set for conferring copyright on editorial work.

There is no doubt that the Dead Sea Scrolls have become a cultural icon. The main reasons for their popularity include the publicity generated by the media, tourism, cultural and political institutionalization, controversy over access to the scrolls, the conspiracy theories involving the Vatican, the role of the Biblical Archaeology Society, and the legal case over copyright infringement. All these factors contribute to the symbolic status of the Dead Sea Scrolls.

Chapter 2
The archaeological site and caves

No one is entirely sure when the scrolls were first discovered, but 1947 has been designated the official year of the discovery. There are several versions of the story and details diverge from one telling to another. One version is that three shepherds had been tending their flock of sheep and goats by En Feshkha, south of Qumran. In the course of their pasturage, one of the three cousins, Jum'a Muhammed Khalil, who loved to explore the crags, threw a rock into a small opening and heard the breaking of earthenware. A different version of this story is that the cousins threw rocks into the openings because they were looking for a goat that had gone astray. In any case, as it was too late in the evening to investigate and the next day was devoted to watering the flocks, the three agreed to return two days later.

But Muhammed Ahmed el-Hamed, nicknamed 'edh-Dhib' ('the wolf'), the youngest of the cousins, thinking that there was gold to be found there, slipped away early in the morning to climb the 100 metres from their camp to the rock face. Once inside what was later known as Cave 1, Muhammed saw about ten jars, some of which had lids and handles, lining the wall of the cave (see Figure 2).

Eight of the jars contained manuscripts and he took three scrolls that turned out to be the Great Isaiah Scroll, the Habakkuk Pesher

2. Caves by Khirbet Qumran where scrolls were found.

and the Manual of Discipline (later renamed as Rule of the Community) and returned to his cousins who were angered by his impertinence. The two older cousins took the three scrolls and two jars that they themselves had retrieved from the same cave and showed them to various antiquities dealers in Bethlehem. There is an intriguing story of how these and other scrolls came to the attention of the world, involving among many others a Bethlehemite cobbler named Kando, the leader of the Syrian Orthodox Church in Jerusalem the Metropolitan Mar Athanasius Samuel, and Professor Eliezer Sukenik of the Hebrew University who authenticated the scrolls. There were secret meetings in the partitioned city of Jerusalem and even an advertisement offering 'The Four Dead Sea Scrolls' for sale in the *Wall Street Journal* of 1 June 1954.

Important to remember is that Khirbet Qumran was exceptional in having been excavated because of its links to the scrolls and not because it corresponded to a place mentioned in the Bible (see Figure 3). In the past, Palestinian archaeology was dominated by the biblical agenda. Sites, like Jericho or Megiddo, were excavated because they were prominent in the biblical narrative. Nowadays, there is a heated debate between those who believe that archaeology should serve the needs of biblical scholarship and those who champion an independent discipline of archaeology of the southern Levant.

For Khirbet Qumran, de Vaux explained that the impetus for its excavation in the early 1950s was the discovery of pottery which was identical with that found in Cave 1. Scholars had known about Qumran for over a hundred years and the earliest explorers (Louis-Félicien Caignart de Saulcy and Henry B. Tristram) were looking for the remains of the city of Gomorrah, well-known for having been destroyed by brimstone and fire because of its wickedness and debauchery (Genesis 19). When they were unable to find evidence for the existence of the biblical city, the interest in the site was lost. Charles Clermont-Ganneau,

3. Aerial view of Khirbet Qumran.

who excavated one of the graves of the Qumran cemetery in 1874, observed that 'the ruins are insignificant in themselves'. Phrased differently, had it not been for its connection to the scrolls, Khirbet Qumran would have been unremarkable as an archaeological site.

Periods of occupation

Like most building complexes that have been used over hundreds of years, Khirbet Qumran was not built in a day. Different stages can be discerned as the site was adapted for subsequent use. Archaeologists differentiate the distinct levels or strata of a site. Essentially, the method assumes the layer-cake principle where one level is placed on top of another, thereby creating a cake or chronological history of occupation, the layer on top being more recent than the one below it and so on.

Within each layer or stratum, the remains of pottery sherds and coins help date the period. Pottery can sometimes be established typologically by its form, material of manufacture, and firing techniques, and it provides a valuable indicator of changes from one period to another. Coins also help to establish the chronology by giving the earliest possible date or *terminus post quem* ('the end after which'). Thus, if a coin that was struck, say, during the High Priesthood of John Hyrcanus I, was found in one of the strata, then other considerations aside the date of that period cannot be earlier than 135–104 BCE, the time of his reign. There is theoretically no latest period, since even an antiquities collector today can have coins of the Hasmonaean period in his or her possession. In practice, however, and so long as the archaeological trench remains undisturbed, the date of a level can be determined by the coin's relative position in the strata.

All descriptions of the periods of occupation at Khirbet Qumran depend upon the authoritative statement of the archaeological evidence by de Vaux in his Schweich Lectures of 1959 at the British Academy. In his *Archaeology and the Dead Sea Scrolls*, the starting point for all discussions on the subject, de Vaux divided the occupation of Khirbet Qumran into three phases:

Israelite phase	8th and 7th centuries BCE
Communal phase	
Period Ia	135–100 BCE
Period Ib	100–31 BCE
Abandonment of the site	31–4 BCE
Period II	4 BCE–68 CE
Period III	68–73 CE
Second Revolt phase	132–5 CE

Israelite phase

The earliest phase of human settlement at Khirbet Qumran is dated to the 8th and 7th centuries BCE, corresponding to the final period of the Israelite monarchy. The chronology is based upon sherds found in a layer of ash, the relatively lower position of the walls, the presence of a stamped inscription reading *lammelk* 'belonging to the king', and comparisons with other Israelite strongholds of Iron Age II. At this time, Qumran consisted of a rectangular building with a large courtyard and a row of rooms along its eastern wall. The round cistern, the only one at the site, also dates from this phase.

De Vaux suggested that the settlement can be identified with one of the six cities mentioned in Joshua 15:61–2, the 'city of salt' (*'ir-hammelah*). Other scholars preferred to identify the site with another city, Secacah, which is mentioned in the same passage of Joshua and also in the Copper Scroll of Cave 3. The Israelite phase probably came to a violent end, as evidenced by the layer of ash, when the Kingdom of Judah fell in 586 BCE, but there is little corroboration for this dating.

Communal phase

After several hundred years, the site was re-occupied by another group which de Vaux identified with the Essenes. He divided this communal phase into three periods.

Period Ia (135–100 BCE)

During this period, modest modifications to the Israelite building were made, most notably the addition of two rectangular cisterns and a few rooms. De Vaux had difficulty in dating this period, since no coins were found. He surmised that it may have been constructed during the reign of John Hyrcanus I, 135–104 BCE, simply because coins of Alexander Jannaeus, 103–76 BCE, were found in the next level of Period Ib. Therefore, Period Ia must have been earlier. Jodi Magness has argued that Period Ia never existed because no coins were found at the level and the potsherds recovered do not adequately distinguish the destruction levels. She believed that the architectural augmentation assigned by de Vaux to Period Ia actually belonged to Period Ib.

Period Ib (100–31 BCE)

According to de Vaux, during this period the Qumran site acquired its definitive form. The Israelite building was greatly expanded by the addition of a two-storey complex of buildings and rooms, including a tower, kitchen, assembly room, courtyards, refectory, dining room, pantry, stables, and potter's kilns. Note that de Vaux's labels are not strictly descriptive. Many of the terms he uses, 'assembly rooms', 'pantry', etc., are interpretations of the functions of the rooms. The water system was enlarged by the addition of cisterns and decantation basins.

There was also a layer of ash and a large cistern whose steps have split. De Vaux interpreted these features as evidence of the effects of an earthquake in 31 BCE and a subsequent fire. In other words, Period Ib began in 100 BCE and was continuously occupied until 31 BCE. The earthquake prompted the inhabitants to abandon the site for approximately thirty years before returning to re-occupy it after 4 BCE, the beginning of Period II. Magness again has advanced a different chronology. By reassigning the hoard of coins of Period II to Period Ib, she suggested that the site was not abandoned for a long time after the earthquake. The inhabitants immediately re-occupied the site, leaving irreparable structures in their damaged state. For her, the layer of ash indicated that there was a brief break in the occupation at 9/8 BCE when Qumran suffered a violent destruction.

Magness' modified phases of occupation can be summarized as follows:

De Vaux	Magness
Period Ia (130–100 BCE)	Does not exist
Period Ib (100–31 BCE)	Pre-earthquake (100–31 BCE)
Abandonment of site (31–4 BCE)	Post-earthquake (31–9/8 BCE)

This modification of de Vaux's dating of the site is widely accepted and has important implications for the origins and history of the community, to be discussed in Chapter 9, as it lowers the chronology of the communal occupation of the Khirbet Qumran site. In a recent article, Magness has reconsidered her view that the site was abandoned briefly between 9/8 BCE and 4/1 BCE. She now believes that Periods I and II should be collapsed into one long phase of occupation between 100 BCE and 68 CE.

Period II (4 BCE–68 CE)

Based on an analysis of the hoards of coins that were found at this level, de Vaux suggested that the site was re-occupied at the reign of Herod Archelaus in 4 BCE–6 CE. Most of the site was cleared and repaired and the debris discarded on the northern slopes of the ravine, but some rooms, like the lower floor of the tower, were left in their damaged state. Secondary modifications were carried out on the buildings, for instance, in adapting a courtyard into a covered space. The water system was also slightly adjusted, leaving existing conduits blocked up and creating other channels for drainage. A feature of this period is the presence of workshops: the potter's kiln continued to be used; a large furnace was built just south of the round cistern; and a mill was set up. However, some of the most interesting finds at this level were fragments of a mud-brick structure covered with smooth plaster which was reconstructed by archaeologists into three tables and two inkwells, one bronze, the other earthenware. These originally belonged to the upper storey above the large assembly hall and fell through to the ground floor. De Vaux suggested that there must have been a room above that served as a writing room, a *scriptorium* similar to ones found in monasteries of the middle ages. This interpretation has been controversial: some argued that scribes in the ancient world did not write on tables but on palettes set on their laps and knees; others accused de Vaux of describing a Jewish settlement in Christian terminology. The period came to a violent end with evidence of damage, a layer of powdery black substance of the burnt roofs, and iron arrow heads. The last coins of this period were Jewish and de Vaux concluded that it must have been destroyed during the First Jewish Revolt, specifying the third year of the rebellion (68/69 CE) as the probable date.

Period III (68–73 CE)

De Vaux believed that the communal phase of Khirbet Qumran came to an end with an attack by the Romans as part of the subjugation of Judaea. Coins of Caesarea and nearby Dora, where the Roman soldiers were stationed in 67/68 CE, were found at the site. For de Vaux this was evidence that there followed a brief Roman period when a small military garrison was posted there to patrol the seashore until the fall of Masada in 73 CE. Only the eastern complex of buildings was occupied at this time. There were extensive modifications of a military nature to the site, such as the doubling of the thickness of the walls of the tower and the strengthening of the north wall. There was also radical transformation of the living accommodations as there was no longer any need for places of collective assembly or any use of workshops. The potter's kiln now became storage for lime. The damaged water system would have required extensive repair and maintenance, so the Roman soldiers kept only one large, intact cistern outside of the building complex for their use. This phase of occupation ended when the last zealots of Masada succumbed to the siege of the Roman Governor of Palestine, Flavius Silva.

Second Revolt phase

The buildings of Qumran were abandoned for fifty-nine years, but were reused briefly and for the last time during the Second Jewish Revolt against Rome in 132–5 CE. De Vaux described the occupants as 'insurgents', but they could also have been fighters for independence and freedom, depending on the point of view. In any case, no actual building work took place. The coins found in a room on the ground floor of the tower belonged to the last years of the war. De Vaux deduced that the occupants must have been insurgents who, being hunted down by the Roman army, took refuge at Qumran as they did in other parts of the Judaean Desert, such as the caves to the south by Wadi Murabba'at.

The cemetery

Related to the occupational phases of Khirbet Qumran is the cemetery, separated from the site by an empty space of 50 metres, which lies to the east of the ruins (see Figure 4). It is believed that this was the cemetery of the Qumran community. This vast cemetery contains some 1,100 graves and is divided into three areas. Each tomb is covered by a heap of rocks that forms a rectangular mound. The tombs are arranged and ordered into rows and are oriented in a north–south direction. Only one tomb is oriented in an east–west direction. De Vaux and his team excavated twenty-six of these from a random sampling of the tombs in the different sectors. Each of the loculi or cavities of the tombs has been dug to a depth of between 1.2 and 2 metres. Where the gender and age of the original bodies can be identified from the skeletons, they were all male and around 40 years of age. In what de Vaux described as the extension of the cemetery, an examination of the exhumations revealed that four of the six skeletons were those belonging to women and one of a child. A few gendered ornaments, beads, and earrings were found beside two of the female skeletons.

In 1966, S. H. Steckoll excavated a tomb in the main part of the cemetery that yielded a man who died at around 65 years of age. A further excavation of eight further tombs in the following year by the same archaeologist yielded skeletons of six males, four women, one of whom had a 2-year-old baby buried beside her, and a little girl.

A recent survey of the cemetery by members of several institutions from Israel and America has corrected several errors in de Vaux's report. The site has six, rather than three, different areas: a north and south section to the main cemetery; a north, middle, and south finger (or extension); and a north hill. Using both surface survey counting and ground penetrating radar, the team found a total of 1,138 graves and not just one, but fifty-four, tombs oriented in an east–west direction. These latter are probably secondary Bedouin burials of the last few centuries.

De Vaux had identified the western section of the cemetery as the most important, noting that only men were buried there; he called this 'the main cemetery'. Women and children were buried only in the extension or eastern section. The recent survey of the tombs, however, concluded that it is precisely this eastern section that is the most important, since a zinc coffin was found there. Zinc, being a rare metal in the ancient world, indicates that an important person must have been buried there. If this is so, then the middle finger of the eastern section was primary, not secondary as de Vaux had suggested. The archaeologists who surveyed the cemetery further bolstered their interpretation by reconstructing the remains of two walls as part of an original square building. This place, it is suggested, served as the mourning enclosure of the Qumran community. It was here that burial ceremonies were conducted and prayers of the dead and eulogies of the funeral procession were given. This recent survey of the cemetery has indirectly called into question de Vaux's marginalization of women and the married Essenes in his interpretation of the now questionable 'extension' of the cemetery. The married

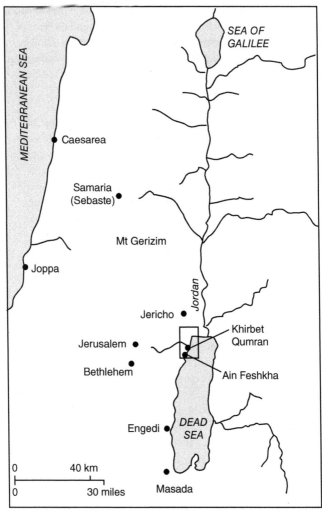

4. Maps of the Dead Sea area, showing location of Khirbet Qumran, the caves, and cemetery.

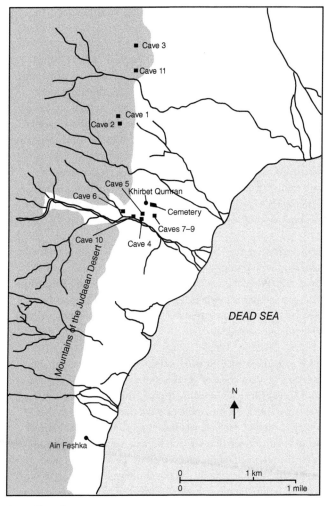

Cave 3

Cave 11

Cave 1
Cave 2

Cave 5
Khirbet Qumran
Cave 6
Cemetery
Caves 7–9
Cave 10
Cave 4

Mountains of the Judaean Desert

DEAD SEA

N

Ain Feshka

| 0 | | 1 km |
| 0 | | 1 mile |

4. continued

Essenes, and not merely the celibate males, were integral to the Qumran community.

Rachel Hachlili, however, has criticized the view of the so-called 'mourning enclosure' as untenable; it is located at the extreme end of the middle finger and is difficult to reach. The building is not comparable to the Jericho mourning enclosure that is built above a tomb and includes benches. Based on the identification of skeletal remains that can be determined with certainty she concluded that adult males were interred in the main area whereas the graves of women and children were assigned to an area on the edge of the main cemetery. In effect, Hachlili's assessment of the data has led her to the view that the community that lived at Khirbet Qumran marginalized women and children.

According to her, the finds of the cemetery are consistent with the view that the community was distinctive in its religious beliefs, a Jewish sect. While the shaft-grave practices shared some similarities to the customs used elsewhere (e.g. Khirbet Qazone), the traditional Jewish custom of family burial was rejected in favour of the practice of burying the individual.

In his presentation of the occupation at Khirbet Qumran and cemetery, de Vaux focused on the communal phase of periods I and II. For him, the Israelite, Roman, and Second Revolt phases were either a preamble or secondary episodes in the history of the site. He believed that it was during the middle of the 2nd century BCE that a group of men came to Khirbet Qumran and installed themselves there. This group of men, as we will discuss subsequently, is the Qumran community of the Essenes. Before doing so, however, we need to take a look at the scrolls themselves.

Chapter 3
On scrolls and fragments

Most estimates of the number of scrolls found in the caves vary between 800 and 900 manuscripts. At least one scholar believes that the number is closer to 1,000. This variance is not due to the innumeracy of those of us who edit the scrolls, but the nature of the corpus that we work with. There is not a single, complete scroll. The Great Isaiah Scroll, containing all sixty-six chapters of the prophecy of Isaiah, comes closest to being a whole manuscript with only small damaged sections. The Habakkuk Pesher, a sectarian biblical interpretation (see Figure 5), and the Rule of the Community from Cave 1, a text prescribing communal discipline, have also suffered relatively little deterioration over the years.

The remaining are fragments of original scrolls. Some of them include substantial portions of the originally undamaged text (e.g. the Temple Scroll); others, one or more columns of writings. At the one extreme are 'scrolls' that are nothing more than individual, tiny pieces or fragments. There are some 25,000 fragments according to one estimate. Others estimate the number of fragments to be between 80,000 and 100,000. The figure changes and is imprecise, because the counting depends upon the definition of a fragment. Stephen Reed, who catalogued all the scrolls, rightly posed the question: What is a 'fragment'? Is it an intact piece of papyrus or parchment when first recorded

5. The earliest commentary of the Prophecy of Habakkuk.

by the editors? What happens when there is subsequent deterioration? Will a fragment, once intact, now be counted as two or more pieces?

There is a further complication that impacts on the counting of the scrolls and this is what may be called the 'jigsaw question'. Scholars have often compared the editing of the scrolls to the assembling of a jigsaw puzzle. In fact, the 'jigsaw question' is much more complicated: we do not have all the pieces of any one jigsaw puzzle; we do not know how many jigsaw puzzles there were originally; and we do not have, for many fragments, a picture on the box for guidance.

Let me illustrate the difficulty of identification and assemblage with an example. Suppose you came across the following tiny fragments in English:

]very thing that creepeth up[
]s kind: and Go[

Those of you who are familiar with the Authorized Version or King James Version of the English Old Testament may be able to identify them as fragments from Genesis and even from the first chapter. The key word of this identification is likely to have been 'creepeth'. It would have been more difficult to identify them had the fragments been drawn from a modern translation that used a less distinct English verb like 'move along the ground' (New International Version). The original Genesis 1:25 of the Authorized Version reads as follows (I have italicized what is preserved in the fragments):

And God made the beast of the earth after his kind, and the cattle after their kind and *every thing that creepeth up*on the earth after his *kind: and* God saw that it was good.

That was easy because you have the biblical exemplar with which you are familiar. What if you came across three other fragments?

]lows Christ[ ]of festival[ ]Jewish holy days[

This is clearly much more difficult. You might suppose that it is from the New Testament, since 'Christ' is mentioned and maybe from a pericope in the passion narratives during the Jewish festival of Passover. If so, you would have been badly mistaken as these are fragments of sentences from Chapter 1 of this book:

> almost always fol*lows Christ*mas or Easter. Of course, this should not be surprising, since the scrolls are religious documents and are of particular interest during the annual cycle *of festivals*, but it is the Christian, and not *Jewish, holy days* that are followed.

The reality of editing these tiny fragments is even more complicated than the second example, because the fragments could belong not just to one, but two or three different, original texts. An editor who is assigned the task of editing them, after careful study, may decide that the fragments originally belonged to two unrelated texts. There would be further editorial challenges if the fragments were once part of two distinct texts of similar literary genre. The three fragments now become separated and are counted as two 'scrolls'. The term 'scroll' can mean a literal rolled up manuscript or a short-hand for 'fragments of an original scroll'. It is precisely this 'jigsaw question' that leaves the counting of the scrolls imprecise.

Editing the scrolls

Faced with these difficulties, the editors of the scrolls separated individual fragments into groups according to language, content, and handwriting. So, for instance, if there were fifteen fragments and eight of them contained Hebrew words from the book of Deuteronomy, then they would be separated from the other seven fragments that may contain Aramaic or Greek writing. Moreover, if two fragments have a physical 'join' where one edge fits into the edge of another fragment, then the two are clearly part of the same original scroll. Note that depending upon what stage of the editorial process they were catalogued these could be counted as one or two fragments. Also, copyright protection is not conferred on fragments that have physical 'joins'; only the arrangement of discontinuous fragments can benefit from legal protection. In any case, these fragments are assembled onto photographic plates that contain other pieces that are related to each by their script and physical remains.

However, there could be more than one copy of the book of Deuteronomy in Hebrew in the collection of fragments. In this case, editors would gather together those Hebrew fragments of Deuteronomy that were written by the same scribal hand. The scrolls, like all ancient manuscripts, were copied out by hand and the same scribal handwriting can serve as a useful organizing principle for editing discontinuous fragments. However, an ancient scribe did not copy just one scroll in his lifetime, so the recognition of the same handwriting in two fragments does not necessarily mean that they originally belonged to the same text. This is not just a theoretical possibility, as the same scribal hand that copied the Rule of the Community, a text called Testimonia, and the third copy of Samuel from Cave 4 also corrected the text of the Great Isaiah Scroll. Conversely, a long text, like the Habakkuk Pesher, was copied by more than one scribe, so the identification of two different handwritings in the fragments does not necessarily mean that they originally belonged to two different scrolls.

One other difficulty is that copyists learned how to write in schools, and scribal traditions and the handwriting of several scribes may be fairly similar, as in the case of the biblical interpretations of Isaiah, Hosea, and Psalms, though the individuality of the pen strokes can be detected by a careful study of the personal styles.

Dating of the scrolls

The study of ancient handwriting, called *palaeography*, can help in another way. From the very beginning, numerous questions have been asked about the authenticity and antiquity of the scrolls, their discovery in the caves, and relationship to Khirbet

Qumran. Some scholars thought that the scrolls were forgeries or had been planted there by the Bedouins; others pronounced them Judaeo-Christian documents. De Vaux responded to these criticisms by pointing out that his team of archaeologists and workers, and not just the Bedouins, found scrolls or written fragments in each of the eleven caves. They were genuine discoveries and not hoaxes or 'plants'. They were ancient manuscripts, and not Judaeo-Christian texts, as established by palaeographical dating of two great authorities, Eliezer L. Sukenik and W. F. Albright.

The scrolls are not internally dated and a method of dating by palaeography or the study of ancient hand writing was developed. The most widely followed typological scheme is that of Frank Cross. Accordingly, the scrolls can be dated to three periods: archaic (250–150 BCE), Hasmonaean (150–30 BCE), and Herodian (30 BCE–70 CE). A date, within an accuracy of twenty-five years, was fixed by aligning an individual scribal hand along this typological and chronological continuum. The reliability of this method depended upon the quality of the internal and external evidence used. Some scholars have cautioned against Cross's method of dating, especially in the assignment of absolute dates to the evidence of the Herodian period and the degree of accuracy of its dating. After all, did scribes not have working lives of more than twenty-five years? Nonetheless, Cross's palaeographical typology continues to be widely followed by editors and scholars.

More recently, the palaeographical dating has been supplemented by two radiocarbon 14 (C-14) tests that were conducted in 1990 and 1991. Basically, the method dates any organic material, like skin and papyrus, by estimating the half-lives of the degradation of the radiocarbon isotope (C-14) found in it. In the past, radiocarbon tests required large amounts of sample and it was unsuitable for the testing of the scrolls. With the refinement of the method, a procedure known as the *Accelerator Mass Spectrometry*, it was now possible to subject the scrolls to radiocarbon test with a minimum amount of destruction. The results of the two tests have confirmed that the scrolls are 2,000-year-old manuscripts.

Referencing the scrolls

Individual scrolls are referred to in three ways: by name, as for instance, the Genesis Apocryphon or the War Scroll; by its sigla, such as 4Q285 (4 = Cave 4; Q = Qumran; and 285 = the inventory number); or by a short descriptive title, 4QJer^b (4 = Cave 4; Jer = Jeremiah; and ^{b} = the second copy of the biblical book from the cave). Scrolls can also be designated by the PAM (Palestine Archaeological Museum; now renamed the Rockefeller Museum) or SB (Shrine of the Book) number, but this usage is restricted to editors. Almost all of the scrolls have these three cataloguing references—however, the Rule of the Community, the Habakkuk Pesher, the Genesis Apocryphon, and the Great Isaiah Scroll are notable exceptions that lack inventory numbers.

Chapter 4
New light on the Hebrew Bible

The corpus of scrolls can be divided into those that reflect the viewpoint of a sect and those that belonged to Judaism generally. Of the non-sectarian texts, the greatest number belongs to books of the Old Testament or Hebrew Bible. There are no copies of the New Testament, unless one considers the tiny Greek fragments from Cave 7 to be vestiges of these books. The scrolls are copies rather than autographs or original compositions.

The Old Testament is a Christian designation for the Jewish Hebrew Bible. The Protestant Old Testament canon (literally 'rule', meaning 'authoritative list of writings') has the same books as the Hebrew Bible, but they are ordered and counted differently. Jewish tradition categorizes the twenty-four books into the three categories of the Torah (five books), the Prophets (or Nevi'im; eight books) and the Writings (or Kethuvim; eleven books), and the entire collection is known by the acronym TaNaK (see Box 1). The Protestant canon totals thirty-nine books, the different enumeration resulting from the counting of 1–2 Samuel, 1–2 Kings, 1–2 Chronicles, Ezra–Nehemiah, and each of the twelve minor prophet books as separate books. Moreover, there are four categories of books in the Protestant canon: the Pentateuch, Historical Books or Former Prophets, Poetry/Wisdom, and Prophets. The Roman Catholic canon includes a number of deutero-canonical books that are not included in the Jewish/Protestant lists.

Box 1. Jewish and Christian Canons

Jewish TaNaK: 24 books	Protestant Old Testament: 39 books	Roman Catholic Old Testament: 46 books + 3 additions
Torah (5)	Pentateuch (5)	Pentateuch (5)
Genesis	Genesis	Genesis
Exodus	Exodus	Exodus
Leviticus	Leviticus	Leviticus
Numbers	Numbers	Numbers
Deuteronomy	Deuteronomy	Deuteronomy
Prophets (8)	Historical Books (12)	Historical Books (16)
Joshua	Joshua	Joshua
Judges	Judges	Judges
Samuel	Ruth	Ruth
Kings	1–2 Samuel	1–2 Samuel
Isaiah	1–2 Kings	1–2 Kings
Jeremiah	1–2 Chronicles	1–2 Chronicles
Ezekiel	Ezra / Nehemiah	Ezra / Nehemiah
Twelve Prophets	Esther	Tobit
Hosea		Judith
Joel	Poetry/Wisdom (5)	Esther + additions
Amos		1–2 Maccabees
Obadiah	Job	

(continued)

Box 1. Continued

Jewish TaNaK: 24 books	Protestant Old Testament: 39 books	Roman Catholic Old Testament: 46 books + 3 additions
Jonah	Psalms	Poetry/Wisdom (7)
Micah	Proverbs	
Nahum	Ecclesiastes	Job
Habakkuk	Song of Songs	Psalms
Zephaniah		Proverbs
Haggai	Prophets (17)	Ecclesiastes
Zechariah		Song of Songs
Malachi	Isaiah	Wisdom of Solomon
	Jeremiah	Ecclesiasticus
Kethuvim (Writings) (11)	Lamentations Ezekiel	Prophets (18)
Psalms	Daniel	
Proverbs	Hosea	Isaiah
Job	Joel	Jeremiah
Song of Songs	Amos	Lamentations
Ruth	Obadiah	Baruch +Epistle of Jeremiah
Lamentations	Jonah	Ezekiel
Qohelet (=Ecclesiastes)	Micah	Daniel + additions

Esther	Nahum	Hosea
Daniel	Habakkuk	Joel
Ezra–Nehemiah	Zephaniah	Amos
Chronicles	Haggai	Obadiah
	Zechariah	Jonah
	Malachi	Micah
		Nahum
		Habakkuk
		Zephaniah
		Haggai
		Zechariah
		Malachi

Copies of Old Testament or Hebrew Bible books account for about a quarter of all the scrolls, 220 copies according to one tally. They attest to every single book in the Protestant and Jewish canons, except for Esther. Nehemiah was once unattested among the scrolls, but since Ezra–Nehemiah is counted as one book in Jewish tradition and there is a tiny fragment of Ezra, some consider that not only Ezra but also Nehemiah was preserved in the corpus. Recently, a tiny fragment has been identified as the book of Nehemiah.

Qumran biblical texts

The biblical texts from Qumran shed light on the transmission of the biblical texts at a critical juncture of history between 250 BCE and 100 CE. They tell us what the Bible was like before its standardization. Did Jesus or Paul have the same Old Testament as we do? Have you ever tried to compare a quotation in the New Testament with its Old Testament source and found that they do not say quite the same thing? The Qumran biblical scrolls allow us an unprecedented glimpse into the fluidity of the biblical text before its fixation and a scrutiny of the 'canon' or authoritative texts.

The Old Testament or TaNaK was written in Hebrew and Aramaic. This collection of books was not written by one man, nor was it inerrant as assumed by fundamentalists. It is not a magical book, but a collection of authoritative texts of apparently divine origin that went through a human process of writing and editing. Each book or portion of a book has its own compositional and textual transmission history. Thus, for instance, the prophecy of the son of Amoz is divided by scholars into Isaiah (1–39), Second Isaiah (40–55), and Trito-Isaiah (56–66), originating from different times, and written and edited by named and unnamed people and scribes.

The dating of the biblical books varies according to the considered opinion of scholars. Those who are more conservative tend to date the books earlier, those of a liberal persuasion later. Whether conservative or liberal, Christian, Jewish, or secular, almost all regard the time of Ezra in the 5th and 4th centuries BCE as vitally important. According to biblical tradition, Ezra was a priest and scribe who was devoted to the study of the law (Ezra 7:6, 10); he received a document from the Persian king Artaxerxes II Mennon (404–359 BCE) allowing him to return to the province of Yehud or Judah with the exiles and the temple gold and silver; he was commissioned to teach the law of the Israelite God (Ezra 7:12–26); he read the law of Moses and his aides helped the people read 'clearly' by giving the sense (Neh 8). There are legendary elements in this depiction of Ezra, but broadly speaking it does indicate a renewal of the study of the law in the Persian period. Revisionists would date the biblical texts later to the Hellenistic period, but the majority of scholars still consider the Persian period as the time when most of the scriptures, in one form or another, were composed and edited.

In the Persian period the Hebrew language was now becoming increasingly unfamiliar, and Jews, whose vernacular had become Aramaic, needed translations to help them understand the Mosaic Law written in the holy tongue. Aramaic is a northwest semitic language originally spoken by the Aramaeans; it became the official language of the Persian Empire. The Hollywood blockbuster, *The Passion of the Christ*, portrayed Jesus speaking in a form of Aramaic (and Latin!). The Hebrew Bible reflects this linguistic transition with passages written in Aramaic (Jeremiah 10:11; Ezra 4:8–6:18, 7:12–26; and Daniel 2:4b–7:28) as well as in Hebrew.

One other important linguistic development is the further shift of the Jewish vernacular to Greek. In the Hellenistic period, Greek culture and language came to dominate the Near East and Alexandrian Jews translated into Greek the five books of Moses as well as the remaining prophecies and writings. A tale recounts how Ptolemy II (285–246 BCE) requested a copy of the Jewish Torah to be translated from Hebrew to Greek and to be deposited in his great library in Alexandria. Seventy-two elders were dispatched from Jerusalem and they accomplished their task in seventy-two days. Even though this account from the *Letter to Aristeas* is far-fetched and there is variation in Jewish sources on precisely how many translators and days were involved the Greek translation was designated 'seventy', LXX, or Septuagint. Sometimes scholars also use the term 'Old Greek' to signify the earliest recoverable form of the Septuagint.

The Septuagint has its own textual history; it was not translated altogether at one time. Moreover, questions have been raised about the source text or the *Vorlage* (German for 'what lies before [the translator]'). The source text was surely a Hebrew biblical text and many of the translations corresponded to the Masoretic Text text-type (the traditional Hebrew text), but in certain books, such as the prophecy of Jeremiah, doubts were cast about the Masoretic Text *Vorlage*, since the Greek version was 14 per cent shorter than the Hebrew and represented a different arrangement of the pericopes, such as 'the oracles against foreign nations'. The Qumran biblical scrolls attest to both the Masoretic and Septuagintal text-types of the prophecy of Jeremiah in 4QJer[c] and 4QJer[b, d], respectively. In the course of history, the Jewish Greek scriptures were adopted as the authoritative version of the Old Testament; they remain so today in the Orthodox Church.

Antiquity of the biblical texts

Before the discovery of the Qumran scrolls, scholars had to be satisfied with studying Hebrew biblical manuscripts that date to the medieval period. The Nash Papyrus, dating to the 1st and 2nd century BCE, was the only extant exception, although it was not a biblical text as such but a liturgical anthology of quotations from Exodus 20 and Deuteronomy 5. The Masoretic Text, as the medieval text was called, is the *textus receptus* or received text. English translations available today are based on the Masoretic Text and most modern ones are translated from the Leningrad Codex of the St Petersburg Library in Russia (dating to *c*.1000).

The Qumran biblical scrolls attest to the antiquity of the biblical books. They are approximately 1,000 years older than the Masoretic Text, dating to between 250 BCE and 100 CE. They are much closer in time to the composition of the biblical books. This 1,000-year period is also significant because it stretches back to a time when the biblical texts remained fluid. By about 100 CE all the biblical texts had unified into the proto-Masoretic Text or proto-Rabbinic text-type and the textual variation was limited to orthographical differences. Some scholars describe this terminus as the time of the fixation of the biblical text; others would prefer to see it as a selection of the Masoretic Text as the authoritative text over against other text-types. In any case, by about 100 CE all the biblical manuscripts found in various locations in the Judaean Desert, not only at Qumran, are proto-Masoretic Texts.

Multiplicity of text-types

'Text-type' is an important concept that refers to the version of a particular document or literary composition. Let us say that you are composing a report or essay; you work on it for a while, and save and upload it on to the 'cloud' in order to continue at a later time. A good practice is to save the document in successive iterations in order to minimize loss in the event of a crash or corruption of a particular file. Thus, you first save the file as 'sampledocument.doc' and having worked on it further save it as another file called 'sampledocument2.doc', and so on. If 'sampledocument2.doc' becomes corrupt, then you can return to 'sampledocument.doc', having lost only the incremental amount between the two. Moreover, you can revert to original formulations and calculations with this electronic paper trail. Each one of these files will share a common core, but will also be a slightly different version. If one were to ask which was 'the original' text, then the answer surely depends upon what we mean by the term. The initial commission of your thoughts to writing would be preserved in 'sampledocument.doc'. However, if by 'original' you mean the copy that you sent off or submitted, then it would be the final or official version of the file.

In ancient times, 'manuscripts', as the word suggests, were written and copied out by hand. The production of literary works involved the compositional and copying stages, with the Qumran scrolls attesting to the latter. As we know from our own experience of copying, such a process is susceptible to expansions, contractions, and all manner of scribal errors. For instance, our eyes could skip from one line to another or from one phrase to another that is either identical or similar. We could misspell a word or mis-form a letter. All these human errors contribute to the creation of different text-types. Other changes are intentional revisions of a text for ideological and religious reasons or mechanical ones, such as the stereotype or consistent rendering of one word by another in the target language.

Before the discovery of the scrolls, there were three previously known text-types of the Hebrew Bible: the Masoretic Text, the Samaritan Pentateuch, and the Septuagint. The second of these refers to the Torah of the Samaritan community who consider themselves descendants of the ancient Northern Kingdom of Israel. The origins of the Samaritan community is a question of much debate; some sources hold that they were foreigners (2 Kings 17:24–34), the indigenous people of Samaria (Ezra 4:4), or a sect that broke away from Judaism in the Hellenistic period (Josephus, *Jewish Antiquities*, 11:340–5). The Samaritans regard the real sanctuary of God to be situated on Mount Gerizim and not in Jerusalem. They still reside today on that holy mountain in Israel and practise their own traditions. Their version of the Torah is characterized by expansionist and ideological readings. Strictly speaking the Samaritan Pentateuch refers only to the first five books, but the text-type is applied to the rest of the Hebrew Bible by analogy.

In the years following the discovery of the scrolls, Frank Cross proposed a local text theory that identified geographical areas with the three text-types. Accordingly, the Masoretic Text was representative of the Babylonian, the Samaritan of the Palestinian, and the Septuagint of the Egyptian location. Cross classified all the Qumran biblical scrolls according to one of the three text-types. For instance, 4QSam^a was considered a non-Masoretic Text much closer to the *Vorlage* of the Old Greek. Yet this text also has affinities with the Masoretic Text, the so-called proto-Lucianic text (a revision of the Greek translation), Chronicles, and Josephus's text of Samuel.

It became evident that the Qumran biblical texts could not be so pigeon-holed. A rival view was advanced by Emanuel Tov which posited a multiplicity of biblical text-types. Tov preferred to call them textual 'groups', but the more common designation is 'text-types'. There were not just three text-types, but at least five or more groups of texts. Tov provided the following statistical data on the textual characteristics of the Qumran biblical scrolls: 35 per cent were proto-Masoretic Text; 15 per cent were pre-Samaritan; 5 per cent were Septuagintal; 35 per cent were non-aligned; 20 per cent were texts written in the Qumran practice. Note that the total of 110 per cent is due to the double counting of some of the texts in categories 1, 4, and 5, and category 4 is a 'catch all' for non-aligned and independent texts. Moreover, category 5 is a controversial group based upon the scribal practice of the Qumran community; not everyone agrees that this is a text-type.

It is now widely recognized that the Qumran biblical scrolls attest to a greater number of text-types than was previously thought. The Masoretic Text is surely an important text-type; it may even be argued that it was the dominant text-type, but there were several others that cannot be discounted. Some scholars, usually of the more conservative position, continue to hold the Masoretic Text as the text of the Hebrew Bible and all other text-types as translational, interpretative, or recensional derivatives, even though they do not exhibit any of the relevant textual characteristics. This 'Masoretic Text fundamentalism', as it is called, prejudges the new evidence of the Qumran scrolls with unwarranted convictions.

The Nahash Episode of 4QSamuel[a]

Let us take a brief look at four examples of how the Qumran biblical texts contribute to variant readings in specific passages from the Hebrew Bible. The version of the Nahash Episode in 4QSam[a] is the best known of the variants that have appeared in the Qumran scrolls. At the beginning of 1 Samuel 11, there is an account of Nahash the Ammonite besieging the Israelite town of Jabesh-gilead. In the books of Samuel, scholars have identified two literary strands: an early source that considered the establishment of the kingship as divinely ordained and a late source that was anti-monarchy. The Revised Standard Version of the end of chapter 10 and the beginning of chapter 11 read as follows:

> [27] But some worthless fellows said, 'How can this man [i.e. Saul] save us?' And they despised him, and brought him no present. But he held his peace. **11:1** Then Nahash the Ammonite went up and besieged Jabesh gilead; and all the men of Jabesh said to Nahash, 'Make a treaty with us, and we will serve you.'[2] But Nahash the Ammonite said to them, 'On this condition I will make a treaty with you, that I gouge out all your right eyes, and thus put disgrace upon all Israel.'[3] The elders of Jabesh said to him, 'Give us seven days respite that we may send messengers through all the territory of Israel. Then, if there is no one to save us, we will give ourselves up to you.'

The transition between the two chapters is jarring. Chapter 10 depicts the prophet Samuel's reluctant assent to the wishes of the people and his appointment of Saul as the first king of Israel (v. 19). At v. 27, it was clear that not everyone agreed with the elevation of Saul as it reported that some, disparaged as 'worthless fellows', despised him. In 11:1 the narrative switched rather abruptly to an account of Nahash the Ammonite laying siege on Jabesh-gilead in the transjordan. We are not told who Nahash was and why he decided to surround the town and cut off its supplies. We do not know why the terms of the treaty are so harsh; some biblical commentators see this requirement of gouging out the right eye as evidence of Nahash's barbarity. Rather sportingly, so the narrative goes, Nahash allowed a seven days respite, as the elders had requested, to find a deliverer. Saul, the newly anointed king, responded to the cry for help, raised up a military force and slaughtered the Ammonites (11:11), thus proving himself to be an able leader.

The first copy of Samuel from Cave 4 provides a paragraph (in italics) that is absent in the Masoretic Text.

> ²⁷ But some worthless fellows said, 'How can this man save us?' They despised him and brought him no present. But he held his peace. *Now Nahash, king of the Ammonites, had been grievously oppressing the Gadites and the Reubenites. He would gouge out the right eye of each of them and would not grant Israel a deliverer. No one was left of the Israelites across the Jordan whose right eye Nahash, king of the Ammonites, had not gouged out. But there were seven thousand men who had* escaped from the Ammonites and had entered Jabesh-gilead. ^{NRS} 11:1 About a month later, Nahash the Ammonite went up and besieged Jabesh-gilead....

It explains that Nahash was the king of the Ammonites; whenever a foreign king is introduced for the first time in the books of Samuel and Kings, his full title is given (e.g. Agag the king of the Amalekites in 1 Samuel 15:8 or Ben Hadad king of Aram in 2 Kings 6:24). It provides the reason for Nahash's otherwise unprovoked attack on the inhabitants of Jabesh-gilead, namely that they were harbouring 7,000 fugitives from the tribes of Gad and Reuben. Nahash stipulated the condition of the treaty with the same horrific form of mutilation that he meted out against his arch-enemies. Gouging out eyes and dismemberment, repugnant to our sensibilities, were standard punishments on rebels, enemies, and violators of treaties in the Ancient Near East.

It is likely that these lines dropped out of the Masoretic Text by the scribal error of the eye skipping from one paragraph break to another, both reading 'Nahash' (see Figure 6). In the account of Nahash and Jabesh-gilead in *Jewish Antiquities* 6:68, it is evident that Josephus had a text that contained this missing paragraph. Some scholars are so convinced that this originally belonged to the

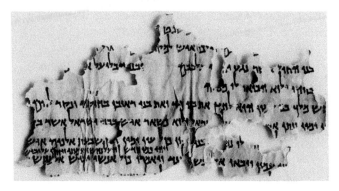

6. A copy of Samuel from Cave 4 that preserves the missing paragraph of 1 Samuel 10–11.

biblical text that they have reinserted the paragraph into the English translation of 1 Samuel. The letters 'NRS' in superscript just before 11:1 indicate that I have cut and pasted this in from the New Revised Standard Version of the Bible published in 1990.

Mount Moriah in Genesis 22:14

The previous example is considered unusual or exceptional in including a whole missing paragraph. However, even the variant of a single word can be highly significant, depending upon what it is. Consider the name of the mountain on which Isaac was nearly sacrificed, which according to the Masoretic Text is named 'Yahweh [or pronounced Adonai] Yireh', often translated as 'the Lord will provide or see to it'.

The Aqedah or binding of Isaac, as it is called, is one of the most moving accounts of human drama in the Hebrew Bible. Abraham's wife, Sarah, had been childless until God opened her womb, making her conceive and give birth to Isaac (Genesis 21). At the beginning of chapter 22 and for reasons unknown, God tested Abraham and commanded him to take his only beloved son Isaac to the land of Moriah and to offer him there as a holocaust or whole burnt offering. The theological problem posed by such a command for moderns was articulated by Immanuel Kant:

> There are certain cases in which man can be convinced that it cannot be God whose voice he thinks he hears; when the voice commands him to do what is opposed to the moral law...The myth of the sacrifice of Abraham can serve as an example: Abraham, at God's command, was going to slaughter his own son—the poor child in his ignorance even carried the wood. Abraham should have said to this supposed divine voice: 'that I am not to kill my beloved son is quite certain; that you who appear to me as God, I am not certain, nor can I ever be, even if the voice thunders from the sky'. (from 'The Disputes between the Philosophical and Theological Faculties')

In the Genesis narrative, Abraham bound Isaac, thus the name *aqedah* or binding, and was about to slaughter him when an angel of the Lord stopped him in the eleventh hour. Caravaggio's painting of the Aqedah hanging in the Uffizi Museum, Florence, portrays the expression of utter terror in Isaac's face and the ambivalent determination in Abraham's eyes. In the biblical story Abraham was commended for his faithfulness as a 'fearer of God [*elohim*]' (v. 12) and a ram was sacrificed in his son's stead. The climax of this episode is the naming of the place by Abraham as 'Yahweh Yireh' with an explanatory gloss that to this day 'on the mountain of Yahweh he may be seen' (or RSV 'it shall be provided'). 2 Chronicles 3 interpreted the place to be the temple site stating that Solomon had built the house of God on Mount Moriah where the Lord appeared to David his father (v. 1). The tradition remains today with Mount Moriah being identified with the temple esplanade and the very rock on which Isaac was to be sacrificed housed under the Dome of the Rock. It was also on this rock, according to Muslim tradition, that Muhammad ascended to heaven on his nightly journeys (Quran, sura 17).

In 4QGen-Exod[a] (4Q1), the name of the place is given as 'Elohim Yireh' or 'God will provide' (see Figure 7); the latter half of the

7. Fragment of 4QGen-Exodᵃ naming Mount Moriah as 'Elohim Yireh'.

verse is unfortunately mutilated. This reading uses the more generic name of 'Elohim' or God rather than 'Yahweh', the personal name of the God of Israel. All the main witnesses attest to 'Yahweh', agreeing with 'the angel of Yahweh' in vv. 11 and 15. It is possible that the original name of the place was 'Elohim Yireh', corresponding to 'God *(elohim)* will provide' in v. 8 and 'a fearer of God [*elohim*] are you' v. 12, and it was adapted by J or the Yahwist (the Pentateuch is compiled according to several documents) to reflect his theology.

Goliath's height

According to 1 Samuel 17, the Philistines had a champion who caused great fear in King Saul and the people of Israel. The Masoretic Text reported that he was a giant of 6 cubits and 1 span, or *c.*3 metres (or 9 foot 9 inches) (v. 4). The main witnesses of the Septuagint and 4QSamᵃ, however, provide measurements of a man who though he was tall, was not of gigantic proportions at 4 cubits and 1 span, or *c.*2m (or 6 foot 9 inches). Many professional basketball players would be taller than Goliath!

'Those who wait upon the Lord' (Isaiah 40:31)

One of the well-loved verses in Isaiah is the assurance that the author of 'Second Isaiah' gives to the Israelite exiles of a renewal of their strength. The passage was celebrated in the re-creation of the life of Eric Liddell, the Scottish missionary, in the academy award winning film *Chariots of Fire*. Liddell, the rugby and sprinting star, who refused to compromise his Christian principles by running on the Sabbath in the 1924 Olympic Games, read out in church this passage from Isaiah prior to his race. The translation is best known in the Authorized Version or King James Version rendering:

> [31] But they that wait upon the LORD shall renew their strength; they shall mount up with wings as eagles; they shall run, and not be weary; and they shall walk, and *not faint*.

Had Liddell been reading the Great Isaiah Scroll from Cave 1, however, the comparison between his running and the flying of eagles would have been spoilt as 1QIsa[a] col. 34 ends with 'they shall walk, but not fly'.

Variants in 1QpHab

The textual diversity of the biblical text is also reflected in ancient biblical interpretations both at Qumran and elsewhere. 1QpHab is a sectarian biblical commentary characterized by a verse-by-verse explication of the first two chapters of the prophecy of Habakkuk. The commentary follows the general pattern of biblical quotation, introductory formula and comment. In column 11, lines 9–15, the pesherist or sectarian commentator interpreted Habakkuk 2:16 in the following way.

> *You have filled yourself with ignominy more than with glory.* *Drink also, and stagger!* *The cup of the Lord's right hand shall* *come round to you and shame shall come on your glory* (Habakkuk 2:16). Interpreted *(pishro* = pesher + suffix), this concerns the Priest whose ignominy was greater than his glory. For he did not circumcise the foreskin of his heart, and he walked in the ways of drunkenness that he might quench his thirst. But the cup of the wrath of God shall confuse him, multiplying his ... and the pain of....

The biblical quotation of Habakkuk 2:16 in this section of 1QpHab varies from the same verse found in the Masoretic Text;

the difference lies in the second verb. The following is a more literal translation of the clauses:

1QpHab   *Drink also you and stagger*

and:

Masoretic Text   *Drink also you and be uncircumcised*

There are two readings, one about inebriation and tottering while the other is an odd linking of drinking with the preservation of one's foreskin. In the original Hebrew texts there is a lexical play on the verbs used. When we read the biblical quotation and sectarian comment together it is clear that while he cited one version of Habakkuk 2:16 (also reflected in the Septuagint), the pesherist also did know the other Masoretic Text reading: he condemned the 'wicked priest' for not having circumcised 'the foreskin of his heart'.

1 Peter

1 Peter in the New Testament is a letter of encouragement written to Gentile Christians in the second half of the 1st century CE. It quotes several passages from the Old Testament to support its message, one of which is Isaiah 40:6–8 which is cited in Peter 1:24–5:

> All flesh is as grass,
> and all its glory as the flower of the field,
> the grass withers and the flower falls off,
> but the word of the Lord remains for ever.

1 Peter quoted Isa 40:6–8 from the shorter, Septuagint text. The Masoretic Text is longer with an additional verse 7 that reads: 'grass withers, a flower fades, because the spirit of the Lord breathes upon it. Surely "grass" is "the people"'. The difference between the two can be explained by the scribal error of

parablepsis, the eye skipping from the beginning of v. 7 to the subsequent v. 9 (both starting with 'grass withers'). In the Great Isaiah Scroll from Cave 1, the first scribe copied the shorter version of Isa 40:6–8; a second scribe corrected the passage by inserting the missing verse 7 between the lines and down the side of the margins.

The scrolls have illuminated an important period of history prior to the fixation of the biblical text to the Masoretic Text. Before approximately 100 CE, there was a greater diversity of biblical texts than was previously recognized. This diversity should not be exaggerated. The text-type that was to become the received text of the Masoretic Text was well-represented among the Qumran biblical scrolls, but it was certainly not the only text that was available or read by the sectarian and other communities in the late Second Temple period.

Chapter 5
The canon, authoritative scriptures, and the scrolls

The Dead Sea Scrolls have shed light on the formation of the canon of the Old Testament or Hebrew Bible in the Second Temple period. They provide unprecedented insight into the process that led to the canonization of the Bible by providing us with exemplars of their biblical texts and how they used them in an authoritative manner.

The issue of canon is related to, but also distinct from, the issue of textual diversity that was discussed in Chapter 4. The canonical question refers to the books that were considered authoritative, whereas the issue of textual diversity refers to which version of a book was considered canonical. Thus, for instance, the Jewish and Protestant canons accept the Masoretic Text of Jeremiah as authoritative, whereas the Orthodox Church canonized the Septuagint of the same prophecy which, as we have mentioned, is not only shorter but also arranges its pericopes differently. The sectarians considered both versions of Jeremiah as authoritative.

Terminology and concept

The word 'canon' derives from Greek etymology meaning 'a measuring stick, a rule' and by analogy 'a list' of writings. A series of Christian councils from antiquity to the 16th century and beyond used the term as they deliberated on the books that were included in the Old Testament and Apocrypha. This Christian usage is based on the earliest lists found in the writings of the church fathers, such as those of Melito, Origen, and Jerome.

Ancient Jews did not use the word 'canon' to designate the collection of their authoritative scriptures, but they did have the concept. When Jews used titles such as 'the book of Moses', 'the books of the prophets', or 'the psalms of David', they imply a collection of writings, which is an essential feature of 'canon'. When the rabbis proscribed 'the outside books', they must have known what were the inside books, but they did not call them 'inside books'. They called them *kitvey ha-qodesh* or 'holy scriptures'. When the Tannaitic rabbis debated whether Qohelet and the Song of Songs were holy writings, they must have known which books 'defiled the hands' (i.e. made them impure).

It is widely agreed that 'canon' is a suitable term to use for discussing the Jewish Holy Scriptures, despite the fact that ancient Jews did not use the term. When the church fathers referred to the list of Old Testament books, they were appealing to Jewish lists. Origen, for instance, listed 'the canonical books as the Hebrews have handed them down'. Likewise, Jerome referred to the three ways of counting the books (22, 24, and 27) in relation to the alphabet and peculiarities of the Hebrew language.

An important distinction should be drawn between 'canon' and 'authoritative scriptures', between the first closed list and the open collections of writings that have yet to be defined as 'holy scriptures'. Evidence of the list is found in the 1st century CE and in the writings of Josephus. While Josephus does not name the books contained in this list, he does enumerate them as containing twenty-two books (*Against Apion* 1:38–43). About the same time, a Jewish apocalypse called 4 Ezra also mentions the books of the public canon as containing twenty-four books. We do not know how they counted the books or divided them into the three sections; however, it is clear that by the 1st century there was

Box 2. Theory of the majority canon

The theory of the majority canon suggests that the Pharisaic canon
became the canon of Rabbinic Judaism, because the majority of
those who re-founded the religion after the destruction of the
temple in 70 CE were Pharisees. Before the emergence of the one
traditional canon Jewish communities had different collections
of texts as authoritative scriptures. The origins and development
of the canon were influenced by internal and external factors.
There was no central body of priests at the Temple of Jerusalem
that pronounced on the canon. Rather the authority arose
from the bottom up as Jews came to regard certain books, but
not others, as canonical.

a Jewish canon. Not all Jews in antiquity agreed with all the books
contained in this canon, as Mishnah Yadayim attests, but there
was consensus as the canonical list in Baba Bathra later shows
(see Box 2).

Before the 1st century, it is better to use the designation of
'authoritative scriptures'. This terminology is a modern creation; no
ancient source uses it to describe the sacred writings. Nonetheless,
it is widely agreed that the terminology is useful to designate the
open collections of writings that were accepted and used by a
particular Jewish or Christian community.

Authoritative scriptures of the sectarians

The communities reflected in the sectarian scrolls did not have a
closed canon. They held to collections of authoritative scriptures
that included the Torah or Pentateuch and a group of prophetic
writings. The Damascus Document's reference to 'the sealed
Torah' refers to the Pentateuch, as evidenced by its citation of
passages from all five books (CD [Cairo Damascus Document]
5:2; 6:3–4). The books of the prophets remained an open category;

there is no evidence that the second part of the canon was already closed. But some of the prophetic books were already considered as part of collections. In the admonitions section of a text called 'some precepts of the torah', the author understands 'the books of the prophets' to cover the period 'from the days of Jeroboam the son of Nebat and up to when Jerusalem and Zedekiah King of Judah went into captivity' (4QMMT C 17–19); in other words, the period covered by the narrative of the books of Samuel and Kings. The Minor Prophets were also gathered and considered as a collection. There was no third section of Writings. Daniel and the Psalms, traditionally assigned to the section of the *Kethubim*, were considered prophetic (cf. 4QFlor; 11QMelch; and the Great Psalm Scroll).

Dual and graded authority

For the sectarian communities, authority did not rest solely on the writings that were eventually included in the canon. They regarded other writings, such as the book of Jubilees, the book of Enoch, their own rules, commentaries, and other sectarian writings likewise as authoritative. The book of Jubilees was an authoritative *perush* or explanation of the Torah.

> [1] Therefore, let a man bind himself to an oath to return [2] to the Torah of Moses, indeed in it everything is specified. The explanation (*perush*) of their times when [3] Israel is blind to all these, it is detailed according to the Book of the Divisions of the Times by Jubilees and weeks. (CD 16:1–2)

The passage calls for a man to bind himself to the precepts of the Pentateuch and not the book of Jubilees as such. The sectarian, however, could not return to the observance of the Torah without the aid of the book of Jubilees. While the Torah was understood to have included everything, not everything in it was clear and the book of Jubilees was required for the explication of chronological matters related to the cultic ritual and festivals.

The sectarian commentaries, known as the *pesharim*, prescribed how the prophetic texts, including the psalms, ought to be read in the light of a subsequent revelation to the Teacher of Righteousness. The prophecies of old were understood in the light of the situation in the 1st century BCE.

> [1] and God told Habakkuk to write down the things that are to come[2] upon the present generation, but the period to come He did not make known to him.[3] And concerning what the passage says: *in order that the one reading it will run* (Hab 2:2d).[4] Its interpretation concerns the Teacher of Righteousness to whom God had made known[5] all the mysteries of the words of his servants, the prophets. (1QpHab 7:1–5)

Formally, the pesherist presented a pattern of exposition that distinguishes between the prophetic text of Habakkuk that he cited and his own interpretation: introductory formula + biblical quotation + introductory formula ('its interpretation concerns') + comment. Unlike other contemporary Jewish texts that subsume the biblical text in their paraphrase, the pesher leaves the source-text accessible and verifiable. One infers that the pesherist understood that his was the role of commentator and not author of the biblical texts.

The pesherist explained that God had revealed to the prophet Habakkuk of old events that are to take place in his time, most likely the 1st century BCE. This predictive prophecy was limited to 'the present generation' of the pesherist's time. God had not revealed to the prophet the things that are to come subsequently. Assumed is some delay in the prediction of the end-time. It was to the Teacher of Righteousness, the leader of the sectarian community, to whom God had revealed all the mysteries of the prophetic oracles.

This fulfilment interpretation presupposes a continuous revelation of God and a dual and graded authority. The biblical text of

Box 3. Indicative logic and the selection of the books of the canon

The selection of the books of the canon cannot be explained by criterial logic. One cannot explain why one book is included in the canon and not another, according to a set of criteria or norms. Rather, the definition of the canon is better understood as indicative and based on the analogy of family resemblances. Often regarded as an absolute criterion of canonization, the divine inspiration of scripture is not a criterion at all because it is a thoroughly human construct. A text's claim to divine inspiration is just that: a claim. As such it requires the validation of a community. There were several factors, internal and external, that contributed to the canonical process, and most of the books of the canon resemble one another in memorializing the story of Israel.

Habakkuk's prophecy had primary authority while the comment is formally secondary. However, the comment also guides the sectarian to a correct understanding of the oracle in a way that cannot be derived from it independently (Box 3).

The sectarian concept of authoritative scriptures was not well-developed, but it seemed to reflect a dual pattern of authority by which the traditional biblical texts served as the source of the sectarian interpretation that in turn was defined by it. The authority was graded, beginning with the biblical books and extending to other books that were not eventually included in the canon.

Chapter 6
Who owned the scrolls?

The manuscripts are commonly called the Qumran scrolls, because it is believed that they belonged to the community of Essenes who settled at Khirbet Qumran. The 'Qumran-Essene hypothesis', as it is known, is still the model for explaining the origins of the Dead Sea scrolls, but it is not without its problems. Over the years, alternative views have been proposed to challenge one or more aspects of the theory. Nonetheless the Qumran-Essene hypothesis, with modifications, remains the most plausible.

The Qumran-Essene theory

From the outset it is important to realize that there are three distinct groups of evidence: the scrolls found in the eleven caves, the archaeological site of Khirbet Qumran, and the description of the community of the Essenes in ancient historical sources. The identification of the scrolls as belonging to members that lived at Qumran who, moreover, formed the sectarian community of the Essenes is a scholarly construct that can be challenged.

In fact, there continues to be debate even about how the evidence should be investigated, some arguing that the archaeological data should be evaluated independently, while others find the exclusion of the scrolls discovered in the caves near the site to be indefensible.

A recent assessment of the various theories of de Vaux's Periods Ia and Ib focused on the archaeological data alone and concluded that Period I is 'unknowable'. But the scrolls found in the nearby caves are also archaeological evidence, and to exclude them is to leave out important data.

We must again start our discussion with Roland de Vaux's presentation in *Archaeology and the Dead Sea Scrolls*. According to him the communal phase of Periods Ia, Ib, and II corresponded to the occupation of the archaeological site by the Essenes. Initially, only a few Essenes settled there, but by 100 BCE the community had enlarged as new members joined the fledgling group. This community existed more or less continuously, apart from a thirty-year hiatus after the earthquake and fire, for the next 200 years. We have already discussed the problems connected with de Vaux's identification of Period Ia and the abandonment of the site. What we want to do here is to ask the question: How did he know that Essenes lived there?

The Essenes: practice and belief

The Essenes are described in the classical sources, especially those works written by Philo (25 BCE–50 CE), Pliny (23–79 CE), and Josephus (37–100 CE). Although there are various inconsistencies and even contradictions in the ancient documents, no doubt resulting from the sources that were used and individual author's point of view, a harmonization of the ancient sources would yield these essential details about the Essenes: they numbered some 4,000 who resided in many towns throughout Judaea and who avoided the cities on account of the immorality of the urban inhabitants. They lived in communal houses in which individual property and earnings were handed over to the superiors. Those who wished to join the community had to follow a two-year period of initiation. They lived as ascetics, rejecting pleasures and passions, and opting for frugality and simplicity in the food that they ate and the clothes that they wore.

They followed some peculiar habits and practices that made them distinctive among ancient Jews. They abstained from anointing themselves with oil, a common practice in ancient Judaism. They wore white garments and immersed themselves in a daily purificatory bath before meal times and after their toilet. Though these ritual baths have some superficial similarities to Christian practice, the religious meaning attached to them is quite different from baptism. They were done for purity reasons and not for the remission of sins. The Essenes avoided excretions on the Sabbath and during the rest of the week they relieved themselves in a remote place where they dug a hole with their hatchet. They were not allowed to spit into the middle or to the right amidst company. They disavowed the ritual of marriage, preferring celibacy to the 'licentiousness of women', although there was another order of Essenes who did permit marriage and sex for the propagation of the species. They did not own slaves, but championed the freedom of every good man. They refused to swear oaths and they refused to participate in the temple service, objecting to the sacrifice of animals there. Instead they sacrificed among themselves and sent offerings, presumably of cereals and fruit, to the temple. Finally, they prayed before and after meals that were prepared by priests in accordance with special purity rules.

According to Philo and Josephus, the Essenes' thought and practices are characterized by their belief in fate over free will. They held that all life is determined by the divine plan. They respected the ancestral laws which included a strict adherence to Sabbath rules, but they were not simply observant Jews as they also dabbled in esoteric teachings, studying secret books available only to members of the sect, which included some unexplained practice of invoking the names of angels. They also studied herbs and plants, a kind of ancient form of holistic medicine. They also continued to exercise powers of prophecy, including the prediction of things to come. Finally, they believed that the soul has an after-life beyond the grave.

Essenes at Qumran

The key evidence for locating the Essenes at Khirbet Qumran or at least on the northwest shores of the Dead Sea is a paragraph written by Pliny the Elder (see Box 4). Pliny (23–79 CE), a Roman soldier and author, wrote among other works a thirty-seven-volume encyclopaedia on various topics, including astronomy, geography, animals, trees, medicines, farming techniques, and various minerals and metals. In volume five, he described the geography of Africa and western Asia, and surveyed the region of Syria before reporting on Judaea. Pliny located the Essenes on the western shores of the Dead Sea in the region of Khirbet Qumran.

> ### Box 4. Pliny the Elder's *Historia Naturalis* 5:17, 4(73)
>
> To the west [of the Dead Sea] the Essenes have put the necessary distance between themselves and the insalubrious shore. They are a people unique of its kind and admirable beyond all others in the whole world, without women and renouncing love entirely, without money, and having for company only the palm trees. Owing to the throng of newcomers, this people is daily re-born in equal number; indeed, those whom, wearied by the fluctuations of fortune, life leads to adopt their customs, stream in great numbers. Thus, unbelievable though this may seem, for thousands of centuries a race has existed which is eternal yet into which no one is born: so fruitful for them is the repentance which others feel for their past lives! Below them [i.e. the Essenes] was the town of Engada [Engedi] [*infra hos Engada*], which yielded only to Jerusalem [correction: Jericho] in fertility and palm-groves but is today become another ash-heap. From there, one comes to the fortress of Masada, situated on a rock, and itself near the lake of Asphalt [i.e. the Dead Sea]. And thus far is Judaea.

This paragraph mentions that on the western shores of the Dead Sea (the Lake of Asphalt) is a single-sex settlement of male Essenes who live without women, love, and money. They only have palm trees for company! Their community is replenished by like-minded men who have been wearied by life's changing fortunes. Pliny described them as 'a people unique of its kind' *(gens sola)* and admirable beyond all others. There is exaggeration in this passage (e.g. 'thousands of centuries a race has existed') and likely errors (e.g. Jericho is probably meant rather than Jerusalem as a place famous for its fertility and palm-groves). It has a post-70 CE perspective, since it referred to Jerusalem as 'an ash heap'. It is doubtful that Pliny ever saw Judaea; he used sources to compile his description of the region. The *Historia Naturalis* was completed in 77 CE and was dedicated to the Emperor Titus.

The location of the Essenes is detailed in relation to Engedi, just south of Khirbet Qumran. Pliny writes, 'below them [i.e. the Essenes] the town of Engedi [Engada]'. But the Latin phrase *infra hos Engada* is ambiguous: does it mean 'down below them is Engedi' or 'south of them is Engedi'? De Vaux held that it must have been the latter, because *infra* in the sense of 'downstream' is used frequently in relation to a valley or river. Moreover, Pliny described the geography of Judaea in a north–south orientation, beginning at the source of the Jordan river down to the Dead Sea.

Yizhar Hirschfeld, an archaeologist from the Hebrew University, had argued that *infra* has the sense of below in altitude and therefore the Essene settlement is above Engedi on its western slopes. Above Engedi, he has excavated and identified what he considered to be an Essene settlement, consisting of a long, narrow terrace of about 300-metre long by 25-metre wide, in which twenty-eight small, individual cells were originally found, and two pools nearby that served as *mikvaot* or immersion pools. He noted that the sparseness of the remains corresponded well with the ascetic character of the community of the scrolls and that there are several other such settlements in the Judaean Desert.

Hirschfeld disputed de Vaux's interpretation of *infra* as 'downstream', because had Pliny meant to say 'to the south' he would have used the words *a meridie* (literally, 'to midday', meaning 'to the south'). While *a meridie* is indeed an expression meaning 'to the south', it does not follow that de Vaux's translation of *infra* 'is implausible'. Pliny used both expressions to mean 'to the south'. Moreover, what de Vaux argued for is 'downstream' in the sense of 'to the south'.

The other objection raised by Hirschfeld is that this section of Pliny's description does not proceed on a 'straightforward itinerary from north to south'. The passage on Judaea begins with the Sea of Galilee and the Dead Sea, continues with descriptions of various settlements around Galilee, and returns to the Dead Sea. It then reports on several places on the eastern shore of the Dead Sea (Machaerus and Callirrhoe) before returning to the settlements on the western shores. It is only here that it reports on the site of the Essenes, Engedi, and Masada. For Hirschfeld, Pliny is giving 'an account of various places and settlements around the Dead Sea from the literary sources at his disposal'.

While Hirschfeld might be correct to dispute de Vaux's claim that the whole of Pliny's passage begins at the source of the Jordan and ends at the Dead Sea, the meaning of *infra* should be inferred from its overall context. The specific description of the Dead Sea seems to pan in a north to south direction. Leaving out the location of the Essenes, for argument's sake, the relevant paragraph mentions Engedi and Masada in that order and in a north–south orientation. The Latin adverb *inde* is directional: 'from that place', namely Engedi, 'one comes to the fortress of Masada'. Pliny concludes the paragraph with another directional adverb: *hactenus* 'thus far' is Judaea. Both these adverbs indicate the southward movement of the reporting. It is the specific context of the paragraph that determines the meaning of *infra* as 'downstream'. The location of the Essenes, then, would be upstream. Khirbet Qumran remains a possible location of the Essenes on account of Pliny's geographical notice.

De Vaux did not believe that this passage in Pliny by itself was the decisive proof of the Qumran-Essene identification. It was rather the convergence of this geographical notice with the resemblance of the communities described in the scrolls and Essenes that culminates in 'that kind of certitude with which the historian of ancient times often has to content himself'. Although de Vaux did not say so, he may well have had in mind the inaccuracies of Pliny's reporting: for instance, the town of Tarichae is to the north of Tiberias, but Pliny reports that it is 'to the south' (*a meridie*); or again, Machaerus and Callirrhoe are located by Pliny 'to the south' (*a meridie*) when they are both to the east of the Dead Sea. Pliny's description of Judaea is unreliable and the exact location of the Essenes cannot be determined by his report. The most one can say is that the report situates the Essenes on the northwestern shores of the Dead Sea and that Khirbet Qumran remains a possibility. What he does accomplish is to highlight that the link between the scrolls, caves, and archaeological site can be established by the similarity of the handwriting of the scrolls, and the ostraca and inscriptions discovered in the ruins.

Alternative theories

There have been in the past, and continue to be in the present, dissenting voices. Recent alternative hypotheses that have been put forward include the suggestions that Khirbet Qumran was not a monastic centre but a commercial entrepôt, a *villa rustica*, a fortress, a country estate, country house/Essene centre, or a pottery factory. Each one of these theories has been criticized by Magen Broshi, curator emeritus of the Shrine of the Book, and more recently by Eric Meyers, professor emeritus at Duke University.

Broshi, a supporter of the Qumran-Essene hypothesis, pointed out that Qumran could not have been a trade centre because it did not lie on a major route; it was not built as a luxurious villa as it did not have any mosaic floors or other internal decorations; it could not have been a fortress because its walls were too narrow and its entrances were unguarded; it could not have been a country farm because it lacked the amenities of comparable farm houses; and the continuity of occupation between Periods I and II suggests that it could not have been a country house before being taken over by the Essenes.

Meyers likewise criticized the alternative theories; although, he recognized the contribution of dissenting views. In particular, he noted that Norman Golb has forced scholars to re-assess the historical circumstances that led to the hiding of the scrolls in caves near Khirbet Qumran. The 'Jerusalem hypothesis' challenged the Essene hypothesis that ties the production of the scrolls to the archaeological site. According to Golb, the scrolls came from libraries in Jerusalem and had nothing to do with Khirbet Qumran, which he regarded as a fortress.

Although the Qumran-Essene theory can be disputed, it does not mean that it is wrong. In fact, most scholars still hold onto some form of this hypothesis with modifications, large and small. A recent contribution to the debate by archaeologists has highlighted the context of Khirbet Qumran, suggesting that the site should not be seen in isolation of its region. Qumran was not a secluded outcrop, but was an integral part of the Judaean wilderness and its network of trading and economic activities. But, as John Collins, rightly pointed out, 'regional contacts do not rule out the possibility of a sectarian settlement'. In Chapter 9, I will describe the Qumran-Essene theory and the modifications suggested by a consideration of the different versions of the rule texts.

Chapter 7
Literary compositions of the scrolls collections

Almost the entire collection of scrolls consists of literary compositions. There is virtually no document or non-literary text with the possible exception of the Copper Scroll already mentioned in relation to Allegro's treasure hunting. There are also two badly mutilated ostraca or pottery sherds with writing that detail the gifting of a slave, property, and produce from a certain Honi to another Elazar. Strictly speaking, they are not scrolls. These were found on the marl terrace of Khirbet Qumran. One ostracon apparently preserves the key term for 'the community' (*yahad*), but the accuracy of this transcription has been questioned.

The literary nature of the collection of scrolls would suggest that it originally belonged to one or more libraries rather than to archives where documents were stored. More than forty years ago, Katharine Greenleaf Pedley, a learned librarian, suggested that the nature and collection of scrolls, which she linked to Khirbet Qumran, indicated that the 'brotherhood' must have also been librarians! They were curators of an impressive collection of books who had to face the practicalities of preparing the leather or papyrus for copying, preserving, and storing of the scrolls. Discussing the collection from the perspective of the history of libraries, she pointed out that the archaeological site must have had a reading room, offices, workroom, and book-stacks. She

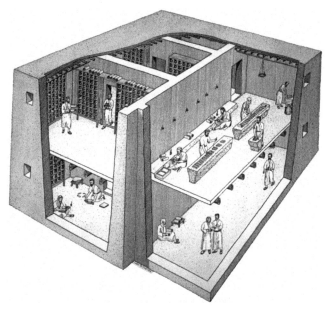

8. Reconstruction of the 'scriptorium' and 'library' of the Qumran community.

suggested that in the era of the Qumran community, book shelves were divided into the shape of a 'nest' (Latin: *nidus*) or 'pigeon hole' (see Figure 8). This view has been adopted in the Israel Museum publication of *A Day at Qumran* (ed. A. Roitman).

Increasingly, however, scholars have come to recognize that the Dead Sea Scrolls do not constitute a single library of the Qumran community. The term 'library' is unsuitable as a descriptor of a collection that is made up of texts from different sources. The biblical scrolls, for instance, are not sectarian scriptures. They are the traditional scriptures of ancient Judaism. The corpus of scrolls comprises a heterogeneous collection of writings, ranging from the sectarian to those that belong to Second Temple Judaism.

New literary texts

These literary writings include sapiential compositions, hymns, poems, liturgies, prayers, and other biblically based works. Some of these literary texts, such as the pesharim or biblical commentaries, are sectarian, while others, such as the biblical text, are not. The characters of yet others are debated by scholars. The Genesis Apocryphon (1QapGen, ap = apocryphon and gen = Genesis), for instance, is a relatively well-preserved text whose sectarian point of view is in dispute. It belongs to the literary genre of 'the rewritten Bible' which interprets scriptural accounts by retelling portions of the Pentateuch.

The Genesis Apocryphon

Take the account of Abram and Sarai's sojourn in Egypt. In Genesis 12:10–20, we learn that the couple went to Egypt because there was famine in the land of Canaan. Before they entered the territory, Abram warned Sarai that the Egyptians will see her beauty, take her, and kill him, her husband. The Patriarch suggested that they should pretend to be siblings rather than a marital couple, so that Abram's life might be spared by Pharaoh. This short, biblical account leaves a number of questions unanswered, including: How did Abram know what was about to transpire? Sarai was beautiful, but what did she look like?

Here is how the Genesis Apocryphon retells portions of this story. Note the change of narrative person from the third person ('Abram') of the biblical text to the first person ('I') of the scroll.

> And on the night of our entry into Egypt, I, Abram, dreamt a dream; [and behold], I saw in my dream a cedar tree and a palm tree...men came and they sought to cut down the cedar tree and to pull up its roots, leaving the palm tree (standing) alone. But the palm tree cried out saying, 'Do not cut down this cedar tree, for

> cursed be he who shall fell [it].' And the cedar tree was spared
> because of the palm tree and [was] not felled. (column 19)

What Genesis Apocryphon does is to fill out the narrative 'gaps' in the biblical text. It explains that Abram knew what the Egyptians were about to do because he 'dreamt a dream', a way of saying that God had revealed this matter to him. He is symbolically represented by the cedar tree that was spared on account of the palm tree, Sarai.

On the beauty of Sarai, Genesis Apocryphon provides a detailed description of her physical charms by Harkenosh, the prince of Egypt, to Pharoah.

> and beautiful is her face! How...fine are the hairs of her head! How lovely are her eyes! How desirable her nose and all the radiance of her countenance...How fair are her breasts and how beautiful her whiteness! How pleasing are her arms and how perfect her hands, and how [desirable] all the appearance of her hands! How fair are her palms and how comely are her feet, how perfect her thighs! No virgin or bride led into the marriage chamber is more beautiful than she; she is fairer than all other women. Truly, her beauty is greater than theirs. Yet together with all this grace she possesses abundant wisdom, so that whatever she does is perfect. (column 20)

It is no wonder that Pharaoh wanted her for himself! Genesis Apocryphon fills out the narrative gaps in the biblical text with this traditional description of female beauty. It is a description of female sexuality that combines physical loveliness with intelligence and wisdom. In the Hebrew Bible, the Song of Songs, with its explicit dialogue of erotic love between 'my beloved' and the Shulamite is a comparable composition, although it was subsequently interpreted as a spiritual allegory of faithfulness between Yahweh and his people. In the Genesis Apocryphon, there is no indication that Sarai's beauty was read as anything other than a physical description of her attributes. The intriguing question is why are supposedly pious members, many of whom are presumably male celibates, reading this material?

The targum of Job

As mentioned earlier, the Bible preserves within its canonical corpus several passages written in Aramaic as evidence of the linguistic change from the Hebrew language. In the post-biblical period and as the use of the holy tongue became more restricted, translations of entire books of the Hebrew Bible into Aramaic were produced. Among the Qumran scrolls are found the earliest exemplars of the targums or Aramaic translations of the biblical books originally written in Hebrew: the targum of Leviticus (4Q156) and the targum of Job (4Q156 and 11Q10).

'Translations are acts of interpretation', as the adage states, and this is certainly the case in the Qumran targums. Consider how the targum understands the main character, Job. At the beginning of the biblical book, Job is a blameless and upright man whose life is destroyed by the whimsical challenge of Yahweh to Satan. Job loses his family and property, and is afflicted with illness when Yahweh allows Satan free reign. At the end of this most ethically problematic book, Job comes to realize that he must repent for not having recognized Yahweh's sovereignty ('therefore, I despise myself, and repent in the dust and ashes' Job 42:6). In the targum of Job from Qumran, however, the righteous sufferer Job remains an innocent victim. It is not the need for repentance, as in the biblical book, that is underscored, but his suffering despite being a blameless man ('I am poured out and fall to pieces, and I become dust and ashes' 11Q10 38:8–9).

The targum of Job also makes numerous changes to the traditional biblical text for religious reasons. For instance, it can flatten out the poetic language in order to avoid anthropomorphism or it can substitute identities that are more theologically acceptable. This can be seen in the speech from the whirlwind of Job 38 in which a number of rhetorical questions assert that Yahweh is sovereign over all: 'Where were you when I laid the foundation of the earth?' (v. 4); 'Or who shut in the sea with doors?' (v. 8). In verses 6 and 7, Yahweh asked:

Or who laid its [i.e. the Earth's] cornerstone,
when the morning stars sang together,
and all the sons of God shouted for joy?

This scene is clearly dependent upon the depiction of the heavenly court, common to Near Eastern and biblical mythology. The morning stars are personified as singing and the sons of God rejoice.

In the Qumran scroll, the targumist was troubled by the personification of the morning stars singing together. To avoid this anthropomorphism, he renders the phrase as the morning star that 'shone all at once'. The mention of the 'sons of God' in verse 7 was also problematic as it may lead to a mistaken polytheism. The targumist substitutes 'sons of God' for 'angels' who are unambiguously subordinate to Yahweh.

The rabbinic targums reflect these and other similarly theological motivated changes to the biblical text. What the targums of the Qumran scrolls do is to attest to this exegetical phenomenon already in the 1st century CE.

Chapter 8
Jewish sectarianism in the Second Temple period

Before discussing the origins and history of the Qumran community of the Essenes, we need to take a few steps back to contextualize the scrolls within Jewish history. 'Second Temple Judaism' refers to that form of Jewish religion, history, and literature that is defined by the sanctuary of Jerusalem. It is the 'Second Temple', because the First Temple, erected by King Solomon, was destroyed by the Babylonian King Nebuchadnezzar in 586 BCE. When the Persians succeeded the Babylonians as the imperial power of the ancient Near East in 539 BCE, their king, Cyrus the Great, adopted a general policy of political and religious tolerance, and allowed Jews and other peoples to return to their homeland and sacred centres of worship. The use of the term 'Jew', rather than 'Israelite', now described the people of Yehud or Judaea. The Jews returned; the rebuilding was completed; and the temple was re-dedicated in 515 BCE.

This Second Temple lasted 585 years until the Romans destroyed it in 70 CE. During this age, Jews lived successively under Persian (539–331 BCE), Hellenistic (331–170 BCE), and Roman rule (63 BCE–70 CE). Only for a brief interlude, between 166–63 BCE, did Jews experience any kind of autonomy under the Maccabaean rule and Hasmonaean dynasty. It was precisely during this time of independence that the communal phase of Qumran began and the sects of the Essenes, Pharisees, and Sadducees were noted for the first time.

The Hellenistic period

The Hellenistic age, directly preceding the period of Jewish self-rule, began with Alexander the Great's conquest of the *oikoumene* or 'the whole known world'. In 323 BCE when he died at the age of 33 without leaving a will, the generals of Alexander's army aspired to succeed him. They fought each other for some twenty years, in what has come to be known as the wars of the *diadochoi* or successors, before they agreed to carve up the former Empire at the 'council of victors' in 301 BCE. The previous Persian province of Yehud or Judaea was granted to Seleucus I Nicator as part of the newly created province of Coele-Syria, but Ptolemy Lagus, another former general whose kingdom was in Egypt and northern Africa, occupied the territory and claimed it for himself. For most of the 3rd century BCE Judaea became part of the Ptolemaic Kingdom. It was only after the battle of Panias between the two warring Hellenistic kingdoms that Judaea permanently became part of Seleucid territory in 200 BCE.

The Maccabean revolt

During the Seleucid rule of Judaea Jews fought to throw off the yoke of foreign domination in what is known as the Maccabaean revolt. A certain pious Jew named Mattathias and his sons refused to obey the commands of the Seleucid King Antiochus Epiphanes to abandon their ancestral religion and to sacrifice to the idols. They wanted to live by the ancient covenant and unlike some of their co-religionists who embraced Hellenism saw the forced enculturation of Greek ways as an affront and a threat to their Jewish identity. They led a rebellion that was successful, and by 165 BCE Judaea was ruled by one of Mattathias's sons, the military leader Judas, nicknamed Maccabaeus or 'the hammer' either because of the physical form of his head or the ferocious temperament of the man. This nickname also became the epithet of his brothers, Jonathan Maccabee (161–143 BCE) and Simon Maccabee (143–135 BCE) who followed him in reigning over an independent Jewish state. Judas was the political leader of the Jewish state. He may also have acted as *de facto* high priest.

The story of the Maccabaean revolt is not found in the Old Testament or Hebrew Bible, but in the Apocrypha or deutero-canonical corpus of texts of the Catholic Bible. The books of 1 and 2 Maccabees recount the story of Mattathias and his family and the Jewish festival of Hanukkah is based upon this historical event, commemorating as it does the purification of the temple after it had been desecrated by the Seleucid King, Antiochus Epiphanes, in 169 BCE. The Maccabaean revolt is also reported by the 1st-century Jewish historian Josephus, whose writings especially of *The Jewish War* and *The Antiquities of the Jews* are indispensable for the whole of the Second Temple period.

It should be noted that from the time of the return from exile, the leadership of the Jews became a diarchy, vested as it was in one secular and another religious figure. Before the exile, the monarch was the head of the Israelite state and the high priest held a subordinate role. After the exile and during the Persian period, the leadership was shared between two independent leaders: Zerubbabel was the civic authority and Joshua the high priest. This dual pattern of leadership was maintained for more than 350 years until the Maccabaean period when the sons of Mattathias usurped the role of the high priest, combining the civic leadership and religious headship in the hands of one person.

What the Maccabaeans did was illegitimate in the eyes of the *hasidim* or 'pious ones', since they did not belong to the Zadokite-Oniad priestly line and were not entitled to hold the pontificate. Zadok was one of the two priests in David's court at the time of the monarchy. Although there is insufficient information about the development of the high priesthood in the Persian period, it is evident those who held on to the high priesthood were now required to have a Zadokite lineage. How this became a necessary condition of the high priestly office in the post-exilic period remains unclear. None of the Maccabees, though priestly, were Zadokite and thus were not entitled to hold the high priestly office. Jonathan and Simon both held it illegitimately. Judas may also have done so; the uncertainty arises from two contradictory accounts in the historical sources of the succession of high priests between 161 and 153 BCE.

Some scholars suggest that the Qumran-Essene community originated from this group of *hasidim* who opposed the Maccabaean rulers. According to this view, these men separated themselves from the majority of the people and the Jerusalem cultic centre to settle at Khirbet Qumran. In one group of their writings, the *pesharim* (or sectarian biblical interpretations), they denigrated the Maccabaean high priest as 'the Wicked Priest'.

After some twenty years of rule, the Jewish people accepted the Maccabaean leaders as rightful high priests. The great assembly of priests, people, princes, and elders of Judaea legitimized the high priesthood of the Maccabaean family during the reign of Simon Maccabee when they declared him 'their leader and High Priest for ever' (1 Maccabee 14:41). This was the founding of the Hasmonaean dynasty, named after their ancestor Hasmonai, which lasted for the next hundred years.

Hasmonaean dynasty

Officially the Hasmonaean dynasty lasted until 37 BCE with the end of Antigonus's rule. However, in 63 BCE Judaea had already come under the administrative control of the Roman proconsul and legate of Syria and in reality its independence was at an end. There were five Hasmonean rulers before the Roman conquest, four of whom held both the political and religious leadership.

All of them took the royal title. The fifth, Salome Alexandra (76–67 BCE), could not be a high priest on account of her gender. While she received the throne in her husband's will, the sacerdotal office went to her eldest son, John Hyrcanus II. The four male Hasmonaean rulers were: John Hyrcanus I (135–104 BCE), Aristobulus I (104–103 BCE), Alexander Jannaeus (103–76 BCE), and Aristobulus II (76–63 BCE). During the Hasmonaean period the territory of Judaea expanded well beyond the borders of the Persian province of Yehud. Not all of the Hasmonaean rulers were faithful to the ideals of the Maccabaean revolt. Some of them assimilated Greek values, an act that their Maccabaean forefathers had violently opposed, and behaved no differently from any other Hellenistic potentate.

Antigonus, the final ruler of the Hasmonaean dynasty, was crowned by the Parthians in 40 BCE, when the arch enemies of the Romans took control over Judaea. For a brief three-year period he was 'king and high priest' of Judaea. But Antigonus's reign depended upon the power of the Parthians and when the Roman legate Ventidius expelled them from Syria in 39 BCE, he lost his political support. Antigonus was finally deposed in 37 BCE by his Idumaean rival, Herod the Great, on whom Octavian had earlier conferred the title of 'king of Judaea'.

Roman rule

Jewish independence effectively ended with the appearance of the Romans in the near east. Rome was the colonial power and in 63 BCE the general Pompey conquered Judaea and entered Jerusalem, the temple, and the Holy of Holies. Having defeated King Mithridates in Asia Minor (modern day Turkey), Pompey intervened in the war between the two sons of the Hasmonaean Queen Salome Alexandra, Aristobulus II and Hyrcanus II, who were vying for the right to succeed her. Pompey re-organized the region in what is known as 'the settlement of the East'. Judaea was allowed to continue its separate identity, but its greatly expanded territory under the Hasmonaean dynasty was reduced to the former boundaries of the Persian province of Yehud. Under the consulship of Aulus Gabinius (57–55 BCE), Judaea was divided into five administrative councils in a strategy of dividing and conquering of a rebellious area.

Roman rule lasted to the end of the Second Temple period in 70 CE and well beyond it. In fact, the rule of Judaea by the eastern Roman Empire, the Byzantine Empire, only came to an end during the Arab conquest of Palestine in 639. Between 63 BCE and 70 CE, the Romans maintained more or less continuous rule. Only for a brief spell did their control slip from their hands when the Parthians seized power in Judaea and set up Antigonus as king.

While the Romans maintained overall control, they allowed Judaea to be governed by the client or dependent kingdom of Herod the Great. Herod was considered a 'half-Jew' by some because he came from Idumaea whose inhabitants had been forcibly circumcised and made to accept Jewish law by John Hyrcanus I about a hundred years earlier. He reigned for thirty-three years, between 37 and 4 BCE, and was known for his architectural achievements, most notably in the renovation of the Jerusalem Temple to its previous glory. The Second Temple that had been rebuilt in the Persian period lacked the splendour of the First Temple, and Herod started a project of restoration in 20 BCE that lasted for eighty years, well beyond his death.

Herod the Great was plagued by domestic misery, having married ten wives who rivalled for a share in the inheritance and succession. He wrote three different wills and when he died in 4 BCE the various claimants appeared before the Emperor Augustus who confirmed Herod's final will in all its essential points. His kingdom was apportioned between three of his sons: Archelaus, his son by Malthace, became ethnarch of Judaea, Samaria and Idumaea; Herod Antipas was given the title of tetrarch of Galilee and Peraea; and Philip also received the title of tetrarch and his territory included Batanaea, Trachonites, Auranitis, Gaulanitis, and Panias.

Archelaus was deposed in 6 BCE on account of a serious complaint lodged by the Samaritan aristocracy with his Roman overlords. There is not much that is known about this complaint, but it must have been serious enough to have caused his downfall. He was exiled to Gaul, and Judaea was annexed to the province of Syria under direct Roman rule. The other two territories also came under direct Roman rule eventually and from 44 CE onwards the whole of the former kingdom of Herod became an imperial province until the outbreak of the First Jewish revolt in 66 CE. Herod Antipas was also exiled to Gaul some thirty-three years after his brother on account of charges levelled at him by Agrippa I. Philip reigned for thirty-seven years and died in 33 CE. His territory was given to Agrippa I before it too came under Roman rule. The Romans appointed and dismissed the Jewish high priests so frequently that the author of the Gospel of John in the New Testament thought that the pontificate was an annual appointment.

First Jewish revolt

Martin Goodman, professor of Jewish Studies at Oxford, has shown that the causes of the Jewish revolt were many, including the incompetence of the governors, the oppressiveness of Roman rule, Jewish religious sensibilities, class tensions and quarrels with gentiles, and social disunity. Conflict was instigated in April 66 CE when the Jerusalemites, who were outraged by the procurator Gessius Florus's robbery of the temple treasury, openly mocked the Roman governor, who in turn retaliated by crucifying the insurgents. The attack of the Roman army began in 67 CE when Vespasian marched his three legions, twenty-three auxiliary cohorts, six *alae* ('wings') of cavalry, and other auxiliaries, totalling some 60,000 men, against the cities of Galilee including Tiberias, Gischala, and Jotapata. Galilee fell and the siege of Jerusalem took place between 68 and 69 CE. It was at this time that de Vaux believed that Period II of Khirbet Qumran came to a violent end as evidenced by the layer of ash and the remains of arrows.

In the besieged city of Jerusalem itself, and even while the Roman army stood outside her gates, there was in-fighting between different Jewish factions. The zealots, who formed a military and political force passionate about the purity of the Jerusalem Temple, divided the city into areas of control by three opposing leaders, Simon bar-Giora, Eleazar, Simon's son, and John of Gischala. Meanwhile, Vespasian had been proclaimed emperor and returned to Rome, leaving the siege of Jerusalem to his son Titus. On the 9th of Ab (a Jewish month equivalent to July or August), Titus took control of the Upper city of Jerusalem and the Temple Mount. The men, women, and children were slaughtered and the city razed to the ground. The temple was also burnt down, although Titus had intended on sparing it. This destruction of Jerusalem is still commemorated today in the Jewish fast called *tisha be'ab* ('9th of Ab').

After the capture of Jerusalem, the Roman army led by Lucilius Bassus and subsequently Flavius Silva captured the fortresses in the Judaean Desert. The last stronghold of Jewish resistance was the fortress of Masada. The Sicarii, a group of brigands known for having used curved daggers (*sica* in Latin) as weapons in murdering those who subjected themselves to Roman rule, held out in Masada before finally committing communal suicide in 74 CE. This is also believed to be the end of the occupation of Period III at Khirbet Qumran.

Jewish sectarianism

The Second Temple period was characterized by the presence of different Jewish sects the most important of whom are the Essenes, Pharisees, and Sadducees. The English terms 'sect' and 'sectarianism' have negative connotations that are unsuitable.

Shaye Cohen, a Harvard Professor, provided a useful definition of ancient Jewish sects:

> A sect is a small, organized group that separates itself from a larger religious body and asserts that it alone embodies the ideals of the larger group because it alone understands God's will.

Cohen further explained that a sect must be small enough to be a distinctive part of a larger religious body, that it must be organized with procedures of admission and discipline, that it must physically, religiously, and socially separate itself from the larger group by creating boundaries, and that it alone understands the ideals of the larger group and the will of God. This definition well describes the Essenes, but not the Pharisees or Sadducees.

E. P. Sanders, a New Testament scholar, applying the sociological approaches of Brian Wilson, further suggested that distinctions should be made between the two terms 'sects' and 'parties' on the basis of what he called 'soteriological exclusivism'. A sect, like the Essenes, is a group that *denies* salvation to all in the larger community. It is introversionist in that it turns inwardly on itself, whereas a party, like the Pharisees, is reformist and simply says that all in the larger community *should* agree with the party tenets.

These definitions helpfully clarify the kinds of groups that flourished from between 150 BCE and 70 CE. The Essenes were introversionists who fled the cities 'because of the ungodliness customary among town-dwellers' (Philo, *Quod omnis probus liber sit*, 76) and that while they sent offerings to the temple, they themselves performed their own sacrifices by using 'different customary purifications' (Josephus, *Jewish Antiquities* 18:18–19).

The Pharisees were reformists who did not retreat from the cities. They were expert interpreters of the law who depended upon the tradition of the elders. They were concerned about food purity,

Sabbath rules, tithes, and the calendar. Some scholars trace the origins of the Pharisees to the 4th century, but such a view depends upon a particular historical reconstruction. What we do know is that Josephus mentions the Pharisees, along with Essenes and Sadducees at the time of Jonathan Maccabee (161–143 BCE) and it is suggested that the Pharisees existed even before this time. Scholars like Hartmut Stegemann see the common origins of the Pharisees and Essenes in the *hasidim* of the Maccabaean revolt.

Whatever their origins, the Pharisees were a definable group between approximately 150 BCE and 70 CE. They were active during the reigns of John Hyrcanus I (135–104 BCE), Alexander Jannaeus (103–76 BCE), and Salome Alexandra (76–67 BCE) and their fortunes changed from one ruler to the next. At first, they seemed to have been favoured before a bad mannered Pharisee named Eleazar insulted Hyrcanus at a dinner party and turned the Hasmonaean king against the party. Their luck worsened when they led an unsuccessful rebellion against Alexander, prompting a brutal retaliation. Finally, they enjoyed a golden age when Queen Salome Alexandra entrusted them with power.

The Pharisees were the forebears of the rabbis. In rabbinic literature they were called *perushin* or 'separated ones', although not all *perushin* were Pharisees. In the Qumran scrolls they were disparaged as 'seekers-after-smooth things' (*dorshey ha-laqot*), an epithet that implicitly criticized their penchant to seek ways around the observance of the law. In Pesher Nahum, they were identified with the ones whom Alexander Jannaeus hanged alive: 'the furious young lion [who executes revenge] on those who seek smooth things and hangs men alive'. The Pharisees believed in the resurrection of the dead, a teaching that distinguished them from the Sadducees. Unlike the Essenes, they did not think that fate is 'the mistress of all things'. They considered some things as the work of fate but others of man.

Finally, there were the Sadducees about whom very little is known. They probably came from aristocratic circles and apparently did not believe in fate or resurrection. Through their name, it may be surmised that they were connected to the Zadokites. Lawrence H. Schiffman, a professor at New York University, has argued, on the basis of an analysis of the halakhic issues in 4QMMT, that the origins of the Qumran community and the Sadducees could be traced to the same source of the Zadokites, though it has been pointed out by Joseph Baumgarten that the Qumran community shared more halakhic similarities with the Essenes than they do with the Sadducees.

Second Temple Judaism, especially between the Maccabaean revolt and the First Jewish revolt, is the historical context of the Qumran-Essene community. The way that the Maccabaean rulers combined the dual powers of the king and high priest in their leadership is important for one version of the Qumran-Essene hypothesis. Sectarianism, which particularly flourished in this period, is important as the scrolls involve all three sects of the Essenes, Pharisees, and Sadducees. Finally, the Romans, with their political and military might, take on an increasingly menacing role in the scrolls.

Chapter 9
The communities of the Dead Sea Scrolls

In his seminal presentation of the archaeology of Khirbet Qumran, de Vaux stopped well short of describing the community of the scrolls. Although he thought that the resemblance between the community and the Essenes, together with the archaeological evidence and Pliny's geographical notice, would prove the Qumran-Essene theory 'as true', he left it to others to elucidate the texts. He was content to point out a few salient features of the scrolls 'on which archaeology can contribute towards the solution'.

The many members of the community, organized in thousands, hundreds, fifties, and tens (1QS 2:21–2; CD 13.1), lived at Khirbet Qumran, in man-made caves around the site and at En Feshkha. The isolated position of both settlements corresponded well with a monastic sect who called itself 'the remnant of Israel', 'the true Israel', and 'the New Covenant', and who withdrew to the desert to lead a common life of work, prayer, and study of the sacred law. Moreover, the choice of the extremely poor areas of Qumran and Feshkha suited the ascetic, religious community of the scrolls. The collective function of the building was in agreement with the organization and rules prescribed for the community. Thus, there was a 'council chamber', an assembly room, a dining hall, a plastered floor on which the president of the assembly stood, and even a scriptorium.

A textual problem into which de Vaux did venture was the question of the location of 'the land of Damascus'. According to the Damascus Document (D) the covenanters went out 'from the land of Judah and were exiled in the land of Damascus' (CD 6:5, 19; 8:21 and 19:33–4). He argued that 'Damascus' should not be understood literally as the city in Syria, but a symbolic name, borrowed from Amos 5:26–7, referring to a place of exile, namely Qumran. Likewise, 'the land of Judah', from which they departed, must also be understood symbolically to designate the priests and other acolytes in Jerusalem from whom the community separated themselves.

De Vaux recognized a major obstacle in trying to reconcile the sectarians of the Rule of the Community with those of the D in that the former were celibate while the latter were married members with children. He suggested that 'several groups existed side by side at Qumran who agreed on essentials but did not have an organization or way of life that were identical.' The male-only community lived at the site itself while the married Essenes lived in caves, huts, and tents ('camps') set up at the foot of the rock cliff.

Finally, he was happy to support the identification of 'the Wicked Priest', or *ha-cohen ha-rasha*, as Jonathan or Simon Maccabee, although he noted that the archaeological findings make it 'inadvisable to go back much earlier than the reign of John Hyrcanus I'. On the question of the identity of the Teacher of Righteousness he remained silent.

De Vaux's views need to be corrected and qualified. First, it is unlikely that throngs of Essenes lived at Qumran and En Feshka. The mention of 'thousands, hundreds, fifties and tens' is surely symbolic, based as it is upon the enumeration of biblical Israel (Exodus 18:25). Calculations of the practical needs of space and water would indicate a much lower estimate of between 150 to 200 members. Some have even argued that the Qumran could only accommodate as few as twenty-five to thirty members.

Second, it is now widely recognized that the two communities, one celibate, the other married, could not have lived side by side at the site. The married members were urban dwellers who stayed in 'camps' or 'towns of Israel' (CD 12:19, 23). Third, the re-dating of Period Ia and Ib means that the expansion of the Khirbet Qumran must have taken place at approximately 100 BCE, at the time of the reign of Alexander Jannaeus and not during Jonathan or Simon's reign.

The organization and daily life of the community

Three scholars were notable for their contributions to the description of the community of the scrolls. Geza Vermes, J. T. Milik, and Frank Cross were all supporters of the Qumran-Essene hypothesis; the main difference between them is that the first two identified the opponent of the community with Jonathan Maccabee, whereas the latter saw his successor, Simon, as 'the Wicked Priest'.

A description of the community of the scrolls is offered by combining different sectarian texts. Vermes presented a detailed portrayal of the community, incorporating textual readings from the Cave 4 copies of the sectarian rules that were released in the aftermath of the 'battle for the scrolls'. He divided the community into two types, the monastic brotherhood at Qumran and the urban sectarians, concluding that the two groups, though distinct and separate, were 'united in doctrine and organization' and remained in touch with one another.

The monastic brotherhood at Qumran

To describe this monastic brotherhood, Vermes drew upon the Rule of the Community from Caves 1 (1QS) and 4 (4QS) (see Figure 9). The monastic brotherhood was concerned primarily with holiness, piety, and the contemplative life. There was no mention of the mundane cares and occupations, but the members must have worked, as farmers, potters, and producers of

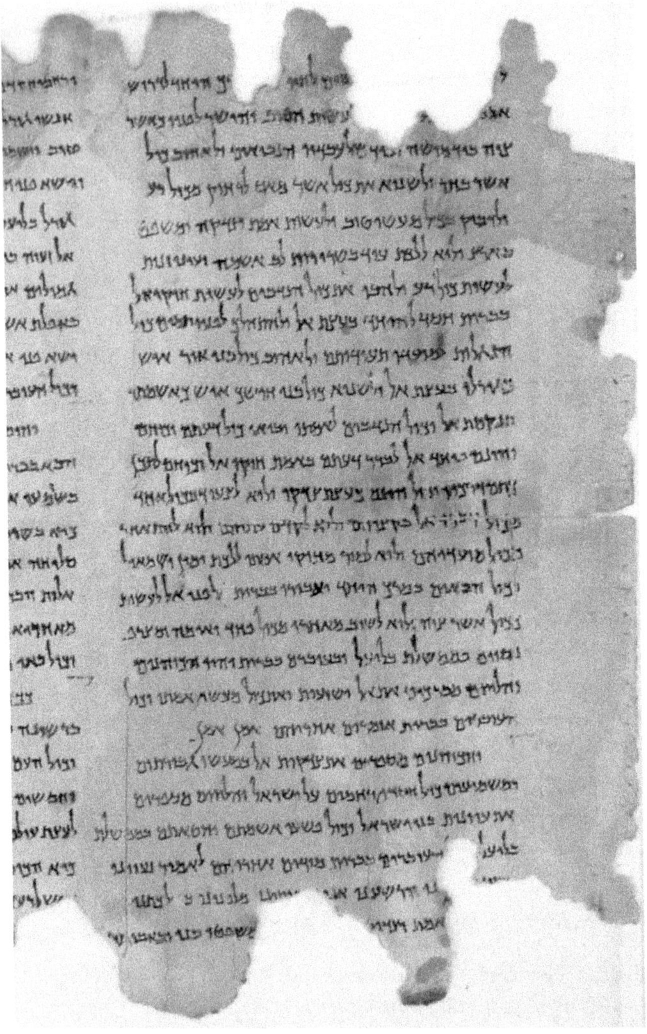

9. The Rule of the Community from Cave 1.

manuscripts. The community (*yahad*) was socially stratified according to a strict hierarchical order as exemplified by their seating in 'the assembly of the congregation' (1QS 6:8): the priests first, followed by the elders and the remaining people 'according to their rank'. At the top of this hierarchy was the master (*maskil*), guardian (*mebaqqer*), or 'the man appointed' (*paqid*) who functioned as teacher, president, and spiritual assessor: he instructed the members according to the 'rule of the community' (1QS 1:1, 5:1, 9:21) and the doctrine of the two spirits (1QS 3:16–4.26); he presided over the assemblies (1QS 6:11–13); and he examined the spiritual development of the men and ranked them in order (1QS 6:14, 21-2).

Vermes believed that the Maskil must have been Zadokite, although the text did not say so explicitly. Apparently the Zadokite priests 'came to occupy the leading position'. This was an attempt by Vermes to account for the fact that in two other copies of the Rule of the Community (4QS[b, d]) the Zadokites were not mentioned. Accordingly, the leaders of the community were originally just priests, but later they also had to be Zadokites. Why the Zadokite credential became a necessary condition of priestly leadership is not explained. Perhaps it is because the Zadokites became the sole priestly line in the Solomonic kingdom (1 Kings 4:2).

Vermes is dependent upon one view of the recensional history of *serekh ha-yahad* (S), namely that 1QS was a later expansion of 4QS[b,d], but this is not the only way to interpret the recensional history of S. An alternative is to understand the Cave 1 copy as the earlier version and 4QS[b, d] as the later, abbreviated recension of the rule as argued by Philip Alexander. Alexander did not integrate his view of the recension of S into a general description of the Qumran community's history, but presumably it could be seen as the Zadokites losing control over the sacerdotal leadership.

The suggestion of a Zadokite takeover or disempowerment, however, would merely gloss over the complex problems related to the reconstruction of the history of a community from the literary text of S. The release of the Cave 4 copies of S has made a straightforward presentation of the Qumran community according to 1QS much more problematic. In addition to 1QS, there are ten copies of S from Cave 4, another copy from Cave 5 (5Q11), and four other closely related texts (4Q265, 4Q275, 4Q279, and 5Q13). S was undoubtedly an important document as it was continuously copied for up to 200 years, the earliest copy dating to 150–100 BCE (4QpapS^a (4Q255)) and the latest to 1–50 CE (4QS^h (4Q262)). According to Alexander and Vermes, who edited the texts, there are four recensions of S: A (1QS); B, which is further subdivided into B1 (4QS^b) and B2 (4QS^d); C (4QS^e); and D (4QS^g) (*DJD 36*).

Can we reconstruct one community from these four recensions of S? Is it defensible to harmonize them in this way? Or do they reflect different communities? At the end of his book, de Vaux had already hinted at a way of explaining the divergences between the accounts of Essenism in the classical sources and the portrait of the community as reconstructed from the scrolls. He suggested that Essenism 'underwent an evolution' and 'contained within itself several different tendencies' as the life of the community is 'traced by archaeology over a period of some two centuries'.

Recently, John J. Collins interpreted the recensions of S to reflect multiple communities of the *Yahad* existing at the same time throughout Judaea. There was not one community at Khirbet Qumran, but several branches of the Essene sect spread throughout Palestine, each one using a version of the Rule of the Community. Collins found evidence in a passage that describes how 'in every place where there are ten men of the council of the community' (1QS 6:8). This passage has conventionally been understood in a locative sense to refer to the quorum of men required for the community's council at Qumran. In Collins' view, 'in every place' should be understood in a partitive sense to refer to different chapters of the same sect throughout Judaea.

Returning to Vermes's description of the community, he suggested that there was a Bursar of the congregation, also called *mebaqqer*, to whom the property and earnings of novices are to be handed upon joining the community (1QS 6:19–20). He may have been the same person as the *maskil*, but given his specific role in the management of real property Vermes surmised that he was likely to have been a separate functionary. The novices handed their belongings to the Bursar who registered it to his account and kept it separate, as they were not yet full members of the community.

The main institution of the sect was called 'the council of the community' (*'atsat ha-yahad*), but the Rule of the Community is unclear about who belonged to it. In 1QS 6:8–10, 'all the people' will sit in their order, each man presenting his knowledge to the 'council of the community'. Here, 'the council' is equivalent to the whole community (1QS 6:14–15; cf. 5:7–8). In column 8, however, the council is not 'all the people', but a select group of twelve men and three priests who were versed in legal matters (lines 1–4). Vermes left this ambiguity unresolved, stating that

> whether they formed the nucleus of the sect as a whole or the minimum quorum of the sect's leadership symbolizing the twelve tribes and the three Levitical clans, or a special elite within the Council…must be left open to question. (p. 79)

The council served in several capacities equivalent to modern day committees, courts, and admissions offices. The agenda for the sessions of the council included items that would involve debates on the law, discussion of current business, admission, or rejection of novices (1QS 6:13–23), the hearing of infractions, the judgment of transgressors, and a yearly assessment of each sectary (1QS 5:23–4). There were strict procedures in the session: there must be decorum and order in speaking in turn (1QS 6:8–13). Infractions are punishable by degrees of severity, corresponding to the transgression, including expulsion, penance, and a cut in rations (1QS 6:24–7.25). Thus, for instance, if someone had sinned deliberately or inadvertently against a word of the torah of Moses, then he would be banished (1QS 8:22). A lesser violation, such as 'guffawing foolishly' in the assembly, would require a lesser punishment—a penance of thirty days (1QS 7:14).

The copies of S from Cave 4 again raise difficult questions about the nature of this penal code (1QS 6:24–7:25). Take the infraction of indecent exposure for which 1QS 6:13–14 prescribe a punishment of thirty days. There is some debate as to whether the sectarian intentionally or inadvertently exposed his private part, centring on the meaning of the Hebrew word *yad*, which literarily means 'hand', but which can also be understood as a euphemism for 'penis'. According to Elisha Qimron and James Charlesworth, a sectary who intentionally 'causes his penis (*yado*) to come out from under the garment' or allows 'his nakedness [*ervah*] to be seen through the holes of his garment will be punished for thirty days'. In this rendering, there are two lewd acts, either in deliberately exposing his penis or in allowing his nakedness to be seen through his tattered garment. Alexander and Vermes, however, understand the infraction as unintended; his nakedness is exposed inadvertently as the sectary stretches out his hand from under his holey garment. The latter interpretation is more likely, otherwise 'his nakedness' would be tautological.

What is more important for our purposes is that the punishment required by 1QS is 'thirty days' whereas 4QS[e] (4Q259) prescribes a punishment of 'sixty days'. It is unlikely that a single community would have had two penal codes operating at the same time. The divergence must reflect a community that changed over time. But how can we explain the development: did the sectarians become more lenient or did they come to adopt a stricter code of practice? The dates of the copies, 1QS being Hasmonaean (100–75 BCE) and 4QS[e] late Hasmonaean/early Herodian (50–25 BCE), are not reliable guides for the dating of the composition. Josephus, however, provides a clue:

> Those who are caught in the act of committing grave faults are expelled from the order. The individual thus excluded often perishes the prey to a most miserable fate; for bound by his oaths and customs he cannot even share the food of others. They have also out of compassion taken back many who were at their last gasp, judging this torture to death sufficient for the expiation of their faults. (*Jewish War* 2:144)

In this passage, Josephus indicates clearly that the Essenes had to adapt their punishment on compassionate grounds. Because the Essenes were bound by their oaths and customs not to eat the food of outsiders, an expulsion from the order would have fatal consequences. Josephus does not specify the infractions, noting only that they were 'grave faults' that required banishment. The expulsion could have been temporary or permanent, but on compassionate grounds and at the sectaries' 'last gasp' many were 'taken back'. Admittedly, this passage is not about minor infractions, such as indecent exposure, and we do not know whether leniency on compassionate grounds was part of a liberalizing of communal discipline, but it does indicate that Essenes would and did adapt their punishment. Did they also mollify the punishment for indecent exposure from sixty to thirty days because it was subsequently perceived to have been too harsh? Joseph Baumgarten, commenting on the penal code, likewise states that there may have been 'a development away from the strict rigour of earlier phases' in the communal discipline of the married sectarians.

To join the community, a person must undergo an initiation procedure. Vermes is uncertain about the period of probation: 'certainly for two years and possibly for three or more'. Apparently, this is due to the vagaries of the passage surrounding the start of the process, and the duration and completion of each stage. However, 1QS 6:13–24 plainly specifies a process lasting two years: each one who volunteers to join the community will be examined for his insight and deeds by the guardian; if he is suitable, the guardian will instruct him in 'the precepts of the community' (*mishpatey ha-yahad*); 'the man' or the congregation will be asked their opinion about the candidate concerning 'his words'; and if it is his destiny he will approach the council of the community but not touch the pure food of the congregation until the completion of 'a full year'. In the second year, the postulant will be further integrated into the community by handing over his possession to the Bursar who will register and keep it separate. However, he would not yet be allowed to touch the drink of the congregation, on account of its higher degree of purity. After the second year and only if it is his destiny will he be fully assimilated into the community by being inscribed among his brothers and in the order of his rank for the law, justice, and pure meal. His property will be merged with those of the congregation and his judgment will now belong to the community.

In Josephus's account of the initiation procedure of the Essenes in *Jewish War* 2:137–42 a three-year period is envisioned. The postulant 'waits outside' of the community for one year while he learns the Essene way of life; he is given a hatchet, loin-cloth, and white garment. He participates in the purificatory baths but is not yet admitted to intimacy. If he proves himself worthy, his character is tested for another two years before 'being received into the company permanently'. Finally, before he partakes of the common food, he must swear piety to God and loyalty to his brothers.

There are several details that either diverge in the two accounts or are mentioned in the one but not the other. Chief among these is the period of two as opposed to three years of initiation. One solution is to explain away the differences by discounting the one year when the would-be sectary 'waits outside' of the community, thus correlating the two-year period in each account. Another is that Josephus was simply mistaken in reporting the Essene ritual. Nonetheless, the initiation procedure is an important point of convergence between the Essenes and the community of S. As John J. Collins wrote:

[t]he general similarity between the two procedures remains impressive, however, especially since we have no parallels for such a multiyear process of admission elsewhere in ancient Judaism.

The urban sectarians

Vermes believed that the D, the Temple Scroll, the Messianic Rule (1QSa), the War Rule, and MMT ('some precepts of the torah') described a community of urban sectarians whose lifestyle was at variance from those of the monastic brotherhood. These sectarians lived in 'camps' (*mahanot*) meaning 'towns' and 'villages' throughout Judaea. They were married with children and worked in business that brought them into contact with other Jews and Gentiles. They were required to observe strictly the laws and matters relating to the calendar and festivals, but there was no indication of the studious reading and interpretation of the torah. They sacrificed at the temple, not something that their desert brothers would do, which meant that they occasionally visited Jerusalem.

From the Rule of the Congregation (1QSa 1:6–18), Vermes reconstructed the different stages in life of the urban sectary. He recognized that the nature of this rule was messianic ('the rule for all the congregation of Israel in the last days' 1QSa 1:1), but nonetheless it reflected actual practices in the community. Thus, the marrying age of the sectarian was 20; a five-year period followed when the male sectarian assisted at hearings and judgments; at 25 he was permitted to work in the service of the congregation; by the age of 30 he was considered mature to take a full part in the work of the congregation; and as he grew older his burdens were lightened.

Each urban group consisting of ten or more members was instructed by a priest (or in his absence a Levite) who was learned in the 'Book of Meditation' (*sepher he-hagu*), a title that is otherwise unattested in Jewish literature (CD 13). Most scholars believe that it is equivalent to the 'Torah of Moses', the title having been derived from Joshua 1:8 ('This book of the law [*sepher ha-torah ha-zeh*] shall not depart out of your mouth, but you shall meditate [*hagita*] on it day and night, that you may be careful to do according to all that is written in it'). The leader of 'the camp' was the guardian who was like 'a shepherd of his flock' (CD 13:9), providing both instruction and guidance to the congregation. He taught them the mighty deeds of God and examined would-be sectaries according to their spirit, deciding on their fate.

Vermes understood the guardian of all of the camp to be the same as the guardian at Qumran. His role among the urban sectarians was slightly adapted. He was not aided by 'the council of the community', but he did benefit from 'the advice of the company of Israel' (*habur yisra'el*; CD 12:8). The constituent members of this latter institution were not specified. He made sure that no social interaction and unwarranted commercial transaction occurred between 'the men of the covenant' and the wicked outsiders who were disparaged as 'the sons of dawn' (or the pit).

The institution called 'the council of the community' of S is never mentioned in D. Instead, infractions and inquiries are carried out by ten 'judges of the congregation' (*mishpatey ha-'edah*), four of them drawn from the tribe of Levi and Aaron and six from Israel, who must be between the ages of 25 and 60 (CD 10:4–13). The various laws and penalties of the urban sectarians, as enumerated in D, included prescriptions for vows, witnesses, Sabbath observance, and various interactions between Jews and Gentiles. Severe punishment included the death penalty and minor infractions would entail imprisonment.

As for replenishment of the group, they drew their membership from within their own ranks; their children who reached the age of enrolment would swear an oath of the covenant (CD 15:5–6). The messianic rule prescribed that the youth who had grown up in the household of a covenanter would be enrolled at 20 years of age and be allotted his duties in the midst of his family and the holy congregation (1QSa 1:6–9). Vermes believed that there was another source of new membership in the outsider who had repented of his corrupt ways (CD 15:5–14). He reasoned that the statement, '[n]o man shall make known the statutes to him until he has stood before the Guardian' (CD 15:10–11), could hardly have applied to someone who had grown up within its close circle.

In any case, there was no elaborate initiation procedure, such as was demanded of volunteers of the desert community. The guardian examined the outsider and the man would had to have been bound by oath to return to the Law of Moses. On the day that a man swore to repent of his ways, he would have to follow the exact determination of the sacred times of Sabbaths, feasts, and festivals as determined by 'the Book of the Divisions of the Times into their Jubilees and Weeks' (CD 16:2–4). This book is undoubtedly the book of Jubilees. In fact, Jubilees 23:11 is quoted as authoritative scripture to support the sectarian view that a judge of the congregation should not be over 60 years of age, because God had ordained 'that their understanding should depart even before their days are completed' (CD 10:7–10)!

The differences between the monastic brotherhood and urban sectarians is extensive, including the location of towns as opposed to the desert; living in families rather than in community; the participation in temple service versus sacrifice at Qumran; judges' condemning urban transgressors to death or to imprisonment rather than the guardian and council expelling miscreants from the community or reducing their rations; the importance of the common table for the brotherhood but not for the married sectarians; the multi-year initiation process of those who joined the desert sect and the instruction on the two spirits that they received which have no counterpart in the camps; and the private ownership of property over against the communal pooling of resources in the desert. Such variance of practice has led scholars, like Philip Davies, to posit two different communities, the *yahad* of S and the Damascus community.

Despite such dissimilarities, Vermes believed that there was a bond that linked the two communities: they both claimed to represent Israel; they both followed the Zadokite priesthood; the guardian was the same teacher and administrator for both groups; the initiation into the sect required a prior entry into the covenant; there was an annual review of each sectary; and, most of all, they both followed the unorthodox solar as opposed to the official lunar calendar.

It seems to me that Vermes's description of the monastic brotherhood and urban sectarians remains *faute de mieux* the basic model for understanding the communities of the scrolls. It explains both the divergence and convergence of practices between the two groups. One can raise questions about various details of his expositions, such as the glossing over of the ages of the judges in CD (25 to 60 years) and 1QSa (30 to 60 years), but the analysis does explain the features that overlap and are distinctive. Moreover, Josephus corroborates this historical reconstruction by reporting that there existed 'another order of the Essenes who, although in agreement with the others on the way of life, usages, and customs, are separated from them on the subject of marriage' *(Jewish War* 2:160). The marital status of the urban sectarians would require adaptations in their way of life. We do not know whether the monastic and urban sectarians found occasions to mingle. It has been suggested that the annual ceremony of the renewal of the covenant may have been such an occasion, but these are conjectures, since the presence of a few skeletal remains of women and children in the Qumran cemetery are no more than silent testimonies to such a possibility.

There are many questions that cannot be answered decisively. Since 1991 and the release of the unpublished scrolls from Cave 4, the primary tasks had been the editing of the fragments and the publication of research tools (critical editions, databases of images, and concordances). Now that this basic work is done, the scholarly focus has shifted towards the assessment and integration of the new material. Before we can fully reconstruct the historical communities from the scrolls, however, we must analyse the nature of these texts and their literary development. The sectarian texts of S and D were clearly not written at one time. They were made from several parts. Future research will require a thorough form-critical analysis of all the relevant texts.

The origins of the communities

Perhaps the greatest change in scholarly opinion in recent years concerns the topic of the origins of the Qumran community. It is still held by most that the opening admonitions in the D depict the beginning of the sect in some way:

> And in the age of wrath, three hundred and ninety years after He had given them into the hand of King Nebuchadnezzar of Babylon, He visited them, and He caused a plant root to spring from Israel and Aaron to inherit His Land and to prosper on the good things of His earth. And they perceived their iniquity and recognized that they were guilty men, yet for twenty years they were like blind men groping for the way. And God observed their deeds, that they sought Him with a whole heart, and He raised from them a Teacher of Righteousness to guide them in the way of His heart. (CD 1:5–11)

There are numerous verbal echoes of biblical texts in this opening section, none more audible than the 390 years of the age of wrath from Ezekiel 4:5–10. If one took the number of years literally and counted the Babylonian exile from 586/7 BCE, then 'the plant root', a symbolic designation of the remnant, sprang up in 196 BCE. Subtract this figure by another twenty years of 'groping for the way' like blind men before the appearance of 'the Teacher of Righteousness' (the indefinite 'a' is poetic), the re-founder of the sect, a literal reckoning of the chronology would bring the date to 176 BCE.

But this date falls well before the time of Jonathan or Simon Maccabee who has been identified by scholars as 'the Wicked Priest', the main opponent of the Teacher of Righteousness. Proponents of the Maccabean theory point out that Ezekiel 4 cannot be taken literally; it indicates a general period of punishment. However, they also claim that the historical information in the admonitions of the D points to the middle of the 2nd century BCE as being the origin of the sect. How do they know that? Once the literal values are set aside, there is, in fact, no positive, numerical evidence in CD 1 for dating the evidence of the remnant to 150 BCE.

One way to resolve the discrepancy is to posit a different reckoning based on the calculations of the chronographer Demetrius (3rd century BCE), as his work is preserved in the church father Clement of Alexandria's *The Stromata*. According to Anti Laato, if we assume that the date of CD 1 is accurate and it is based on Demetrius' chronology, which is 26/27 years shorter than the historical date, then we arrive at the date of 150 BCE.

Yet another reconciliation is to suppose that CD 1 does not follow Demetrius but rather another chronology, found in a 1st century CE apocalyptic text called the Second Book of Baruch. According to Emile Puech, the D follows the chronology of 2 Baruch 1:1f that dates the first siege of Jerusalem to 572 BCE, rather than 586/7 BCE, and the second siege ten years later, to 562 BCE. Combining this reckoning with the 390 plus twenty years of CD 1, then the founding of the Qumran community is 152 BCE.

There is, however, no evidence that CD 1 followed either the chronology of Demetrius or 2 Baruch. Chronology in this period is notoriously inaccurate. The dating of the foundation of the community in the Maccabean period on the basis of CD 1 is thus called into question.

Another way that the Maccabaean theory pegs the emergence of the sect to the revolt against the Seleucids is by the identification of the leader of the opponents of the sect. 'The Wicked Priest' is the negative sobriquet that the Pesharim attach to the antagonist of the community. The *hasidim* or 'pious ones', so the theory goes, saw the accession of Jonathan or Simon Maccabee to the pontificate as illegitimate because he was not Zadokite. Yet at least one recension of S does not include any reference to the Zadokites. Moreover, as John J. Collins pointed out, the issue of illegitimate accession is not a concern of the scrolls themselves; neither the Rule of the Community nor the D treats this as an issue. The question of the illegitimate accession is derived from the *hasidim*'s rejection of Judas for Alcimus in the external account of 1 Maccabees 7:14ff.

In recent years, a rival theory has attracted much attention. According to the Groningen Hypothesis of Florentino Garcia-Martinez and the late Adam van der Woude (both scholars used to work in the Dutch city of Groningen) the formative period of the Qumran community may be dated prior to the religious crisis precipitated by Antiochus Epiphanes in 175 BCE. The origins of the Essenes and the formative period of the Qumran community are indistinguishable. Both are situated in Palestine and are rooted in the apocalyptic movement of the post-exilic Judaism, as attested by the birth of a group at the end of the third period in 1 Enoch 90.

The Groningen Hypothesis posits a relationship between the Essenes, the Qumran community, and the Therapeutae, another Jewish sect based in northern Egypt. Accordingly, the Essenes belonged to the mother community and the Qumranians and Therapeutae were daughter sects. This explains well the similarities and differences between the three groups. Useful too is the distinction that the Groningen Hypothesis draws between 'the Wicked Priest' and 'the liar'; they were not one and the same person, but two different opponents of the Qumran sect: the former was the disreputable high priest and the latter a rival teacher of the law. Less persuasive is the Groningen Hypothesis' suggestion that 'the Wicked Priest' is a title not for one person, but six high priests in sequential order.

It seems to me that the lower dating of the communal phase of the archaeological site of Khirbet Qumran to 100 BCE from 135–100 BCE, as discussed in Chapter 2, raises fundamental questions about the history of the sect in the Maccabean period. It is in the 1st century BCE, rather than second, that the origins of the communities should be sought.

Chapter 10
The religious beliefs of the sectarian communities

Before describing some of the important teachings of the sectarians, it is important to realize from the outset that Judaism is not a creedal religion like Christianity. It does not require assent to a set of creeds and doctrines. It is a way of life, conformity to a pattern of practices, and membership in the Jewish people. Until Maimonides articulated the thirteen principles of faith in the Middle Ages, traditional Judaism did not have a common set of faith statements.

Judaism is also unsystematic; it does not have a tradition of 'systematic theology', discussing such topics as knowledge of God, resurrection, the after-life, and so on in a coherent manner. The enormous body of rabbinic literature, for instance, does not contain a single tractate or section that outlines Jewish beliefs. As Ephraim Urbach stated,

> [c]ommon to all the sources is the fact that none of them provides
> [a] systematic treatment of the subject of beliefs and conceptions,
> and there are almost no continuous discourses dealing with a
> single theme.

But there were indeed common beliefs, even if the religious ideas have to be teased out of innumerable details of the law.

Doctrine of the two spirits

In the sectarian Dead Sea Scrolls, the teachings are similarly scattered here, there, and everywhere. There is, however, one passage from the Rule of the Community that is an exception. It comes closest to a 'systematic' treatment of the religious ideas of the sect. In what is known as the 'teaching of the two spirits', the Maskil instructs all the sons of light about the character of men, their spirits, deeds and concomitant punishment or reward (1QS 3:13–4.25). It begins:

> From the God of Knowledge comes all that is and shall be. Before ever they existed He established their whole design, and when as ordained for them, they come into being, it is in accord with His glorious design that they accomplish their task without change. (lines 15–16)

The determinism expressed here is corroborated by Josephus who reports that in comparison to the Sadducees who do not recognize fate or to the Pharisees, who held that some events are preordained while others are not, the Essenes 'make Fate mistress of all and say that nothing comes to pass for humans unless Fate has so voted' (*Antiquities of the Jews* 13:171–2).

In the teaching of the two spirits God is said to have divided man into two groups according to the spirit that he has inspired in him. Those who have the spirit of injustice belong to the darkness and are led by the Angel of Darkness, whereas those who are of the light have a spirit of truth and are ruled by the Prince of Light. The separation of all humanity into two groups is often described as 'ethical dualism'; it is based upon a deterministic view of life. Even if the Angel of Darkness should lead one of the children of righteousness astray, this apostasy would have been done 'in accordance with the mysteries of God' (3.20–3).

The dualism expressed in the teaching of the two spirits has a cosmic, human, and spiritual dimension: the Prince of Light is opposed by the Angel of Darkness; humans are divided into those who 'spring from a fountain of light' and those 'born of injustice from a source of darkness'; and the two spirits of truth and injustice struggle 'in the hearts of men'. It is the destiny of the sectarian to belong to the sons of light and each member's spiritual value can be determined by his physical appearance as described in a sectarian, physiognomic text.

The 4Q186 scroll is a fascinating text that characterizes a man's inner spirit by his outward physical appearance. This text was written in code that consists of letters of the Hebrew and Greek alphabets, as well as other cryptic signs, written backwards and in mirror image. When deciphered, the fragments describe three different physical specimens, and the amount of spiritual light and darkness found in each of them. Each man's spiritual value totals nine, an arbitrary and uneven number that would preclude a balance of equal measure between light and darkness. The first man is wicked:

> and his head…[and his cheeks are] fat. His teeth are of uneven length. His fingers are thick, and his thighs are thick and very hairy, each one. His toes are thick and short. His spirit consists of eight [parts] in the House of Darkness and one from the House of Light…. (fragment 1)

A second archetype is good:

> His eyes are black and glowing…. His voice is gentle. His teeth are fine and well aligned. He is neither tall, nor short…And his fingers are thin and long. And his thighs are smooth…[and his toes] are well aligned. His spirit consists of eight [parts] [in the House of Light, of] the second Column, and one [in the House of Darkness]. (fragment 2)

Finally, the third man falls somewhere in between:

> and his thighs are long and lean, and his toes are thin and long. He
> is of the second Column. His spirit consists of six [parts] in the
> House of Light and three in the Pit of Darkness. (fragment 1)

The equation of spiritual value with desirable, physical attributes
may seem to us, at first glance, rather bizarre, but it is, in fact,
not so different from the way we judge people on first impression.
The Qumran community used this method to vet potential
volunteers who wished to join its ranks.

In the final age, truth will arise in the world forever and God will
purify man's spirit and deeds, for 'God has chosen them for an
everlasting Covenant and all the glory of Adam shall be theirs'
(4:22–3). The triumph of truth is accompanied, as it were, by
'paradise regained'.

The climax of this spiritual history of man alludes to two important,
related concepts of divine election and covenant. All ancient Jews, so
far as we can surmise, believe that they belong to the chosen people
and this election is confirmed by the establishment of covenants (or
solemn agreements) throughout biblical history, between Yahweh
and individuals or Israel the people: covenants were established
with Noah after the Flood (Genesis 9:1–17); with Abraham as the
father of many nations (Genesis 15, 17:1–4); with Israel as the
people of God (Exodus 19–24); with Phinehas (Numbers 25); with
Levi (Malachi 2:4–5); and with the davidic kingship (2 Samuel 7;
Psalms 78:67–72). This covenantal relationship can be
unconditional and everlasting or it can require the obedience of
divine commandments with punishment for transgressions.

In the course of history, however, Israel often strayed and
prophets were raised to proclaim the message of repentance. One
development of this covenantal relationship that is particularly

important for the sectarians is the notion of the remnant or true Israel. Remnant theology postulates a nucleus of Israel who remains faithful to Yahweh. In the biblical text 'remnant' means a vestige of survivors after destruction, typified by Noah and his family (Genesis 7:23). Theologizing this notion, the prophetic writings invested 'the remnant' with the added belief of a hope of for the future (Isaiah 10:20-1).

The new covenant

Jeremiah 31:31-4 should be singled out as a biblical passage of fundamental importance for the sectarians, for in it is expressed the view that Yahweh has established a 'new covenant with the house of Israel and the house of Judah' (v. 31). The innovation of this covenant is to be found in the belief that the law will be placed within men, written upon their hearts. By declaring this new dispensation, the passage remarkably advocates a setting aside of the teaching of the torah (v. 34). It is no wonder that the antinomian tendencies of the Pauline letters take up this point.

The sectarian scrolls mention the 'new covenant' several times; explicitly referring to Jeremiah as the source in CD 8:20-1 (cf. Ms B 19:33-5). However, the 'new covenant' (*berit hadasha*) here should be understood as 'the renewed covenant'. Shemaryahu Talmon insightfully observed that the covenant mentioned was the ancient, ancestral one. Consider the opening words of the Damascus Document:

> Listen now all you who know righteousness, and consider the works of God; for He has a dispute with all flesh and will condemn all those who despise Him. For when they were unfaithful and forsook Him, He hid His face from Israel and His Sanctuary and delivered them up to the sword. But remembering the Covenant of the forefathers, He left a remnant to Israel and did not deliver it up to be destroyed. (CD 1:1-5)

In other words, while the sectarians use the phrase 'the new covenant', they do not understand it in the New Testament sense of a new dispensation or stage in the unfolding of the divine will. Rather 'new' has the sense of 'renewal'.

The classical sources do not mention the new covenant or the remnant in relation to the Essenes. This should not be surprising since Josephus and Philo's readership was Greek and primarily non-Jewish. The former, for instance, referred to the Pythagoreans (*AJ* 15:371) and the Dacians (*AJ* 18:22) in order to compare them to the Essenes. Josephus reports only that the Essenes revered their ancestral laws (*JW* 2:159) and Philo their biblical interpretation 'by symbols' (*Quod ominis probus liber sit* 82).

Thanks to the sectarian scrolls we now know far more about Jewish religious beliefs in the Second Temple period, particularly between 200 BCE and 70 CE, than we did previously. The scrolls give us an insight into the flourishing of sectarianism and provided us with the actual documents of one of its sects, the Essenes.

Chapter 11
The scrolls and early Christianity

If media attention and sales figures are anything to go by, then the most sensational aspects of research are related to the link between the scrolls and the origins of the early Church. As mentioned in the opening chapter, even a whiff of controversy, especially involving the Vatican, will send journalists scurrying to investigate. The appetite of the public for plots involving the Dead Sea Scrolls remains unabated; secrecy, back-room deals, and spin-doctoring appeal to the human psyche that seeks to glimpse into a covert world of political and religious machinations beneath the ordered and institutionalized edifice of established religion.

One does not have to look very far to find such sensational claims. Take the book by Barbara Thiering, *Jesus the Man* (1992), which has been a bestseller. It purports to show that Jesus did not die on the Cross but survived, married Mary Magdalene, and fathered several children. The book is based on Thiering's understanding of the pesher method which she uses to decode the Gospel stories. Apart from the coincidence of evoking the Hebrew word, her method bears little resemblance to the pesher method as was practised by the community. The ancient sectarians understood prophetic texts of old to foretell events that were taking place during their time. Thus, for instance, those who were called 'the Chaldeans' in the Habakkuk's prophecy were identified with 'the Kittim' (the Romans) of their time who took control of the ancient

Near East in 63 BCE. By contrast, Thiering understands pesher as a literalistic method of decoding the words of the New Testament to reveal a hidden, secret meaning that she uses arbitrarily to reconstruct an alternative history of the 1st-century CE world.

New Testament scrolls?

Thiering's book is primarily based upon an oblique use of the Qumran scrolls; she utilizes a method that she purportedly finds in the sectarian biblical commentaries for her exegesis of the Gospels. Other scholars have been more direct, either by positing that some of the scrolls are in fact New Testament documents or that they attest to a messianic figure like Jesus.

In 1992, Carsten Peter Thiede published a study of two tiny fragments and claimed that they were New Testament texts. Cave 7 is unusual in having preserved only Greek texts, and Thiede has revived the view, first suggested by José O'Callaghan in the 1970s, that two of these fragments, 7Q5 and 7Q4, could be identified as Mark 6:52–3 and 1 Timothy 3:16–4:3, respectively. The larger of these two fragments, 7Q5, preserves no more than twenty partial or whole letters. It contains only one full word, *kai* the Greek for 'and' (see Figure 10). Despite the paucity of its preservation and the ostensible lack of distinctive features, Thiede argued that 7Q5 could be reconstructed as part of the Gospel pericope depicting Jesus's miraculous walking on the water of the Sea of Galilee or Lake Genessaret as found at the end of Mark 6. Thiede translated 7Q5 as follows:

> ... understood about the loaves; their hearts were hardened. And when they had crossed over, they landed at Gennesaret and anchored there. And when they got ...

To do so he has to posit an unattested textual variant; against all other witnesses 7Q5 did not read *epi ten gen*, the Greek adverbial phrase meaning 'to the land [or shore]', to complement the verb

10. Fragment with Greek letters from Cave 7.

'anchored'. Moreover, the original Greek verb of 'they had crossed over' required an initial sound shift from a letter delta to a tau, *diaperassantes* to *tiaperassantes*. The most questionable of Thiede's assumptions is that the stichometry or line-length of 7Q5 is between twenty and twenty-three letters even when the right and left margins are not preserved in any of the five lines. Thiede followed O'Callaghan in calculating the number of letters by comparing 7Q5 to 7Q1 (= Exodus 28:4–7) and 7Q2 (= Letter of Jeremiah 6:43–4) that have line-lengths of between sixteen and twenty-three letters. This is a highly dubious procedure. Just because the three fragments were found in the same cave does not in any way justify the assumption that they had similar column widths. Various texts have different column widths, even those that were copied on the same scroll. Other scholars have identified the same fragments as the Greek texts of 1 Enoch. Prudence should guide one to be cautious in reading so much significance out of so little evidence.

The 'slain messiah' text

As mentioned in the opening chapter, one of the best-publicized claims in the aftermath of 'the battle for the scrolls' was the discovery of a text that apparently depicted a dying messianic figure. The relevant text is 4Q285, fragment 5 (now renumbered to 7). There are six lines to this badly mutilated fragment:

> [1] [As it is written in the book of] Isaiah the Prophet, [The thickets of the forest] will be cut [down with an axe and Lebanon by a majestic one [2] will f]all. And there shall come forth a shoot from the stump of Jesse [...] [3] the Branch of David and they will enter into judgement with [...] [4] and the Prince of the Congregation, the Br[anch of David] will kill him [...[5] by strok]es and by wounds. And a Priest [of renown (?)] will command[6] [... the s]lai[n] of the Kitti[m ...]

Michael Wise and Robert Eisenman had suggested to the media that this fragment depicted a dying or slain messiah. Their proposal, so far as I know, was never published in a scholarly journal. The 4Q285 scroll, as we now know, is a rule of war, containing some ten fragments. The translation reflects the present scholarly consensus. At the time in 1991, the dispute centred on the reading of line 4. Wise and Eisenman suggested that it meant 'and they will kill the Prince of the Congregation', a figure known elsewhere in the scrolls and who in this passage is related to the messianic proclamation of Isaiah 10:34–11.1. However, the Oxford seminar, as mentioned in Chapter 1, concluded that it ought to read 'and the Prince of the Congregation will kill him', that is to say the messianic prince will not be put to death; rather he will kill someone else, an unknown victim.

How is it possible to have such opposite interpretations? In order to understand the difficulties, it is important to note that the Hebrew of the Dead Sea Scrolls is unpointed or unvocalized. This means that only consonants are written, although there are 'reading aids' called *matres lectionis* ('mothers of reading'). It would be a similar experience to reading the following English sentence written only with consonants and 'y's:

my lvs lk rd rd rs thts nwly sprng n jn

For:

My luve's like a red, red rose that's newly sprung in June

This lack of vocalization could lead to ambiguity. Take the consonants, 'rd', as an example. It could be vocalized as 'red', 'ride', 'rode', 'rod', 'rood', 'road', 'raid', 'reed', etc. Hebrew grammar also has another feature that has no counterpart in the English language and that is the ability to add suffixes, whether objective or subjective, directly on to the end of a verb.

In the fragment of 4Q285, the verb for 'to put to death', with the consonants *hmytw*, can be pointed *hemytu*, rendering the final either as a vowel 'u' of the third person plural or alternatively *hemyto*, taking the 'w' as the objective suffix 'o' or 'him'. The former would yield a sentence meaning 'they will kill (or killed) the Prince of the Congregation' and the latter, 'the Prince of the Congregation will kill (or killed) him'. Because the verb is also preceded by a conjunction, there is further ambiguity about whether it should be translated in the past or future tense.

Grammatically, both readings are possible. The main reason that the one is more probable than the other is that in all other passages in the scrolls where the Prince of the Congregation is mentioned he is depicted as the triumphant messianic figure. In fact in 4QpIsa^a, a pesher to Isaiah, and 1QSb, the rule of blessings, the Prince of the Congregation is depicted as the triumphant figure that fulfils the very same biblical prophecy of Isaiah 10–11.

Common sectarian matrix

These are two failed attempts to establish a direct link between the scrolls and Christianity. Over the years, several others have been advanced and were no more persuasive. It seems to me that there is a better model and that is to regard the Essenes, the Qumran community of the *yahad*, the urban sectarians, the Jerusalem church, and the Pauline congregations as distinct groups that shared a common sectarian matrix. There were other groups beside. This sectarian matrix includes separation from the majority, organization into groups, religious ideas, and the choice of favourite biblical proof-texts that legitimize a sect's existence. The groups drew inspiration from the biblical texts; in doing so, they shared this common heritage with other Jews in the late Second Temple period. But they were also sectarians—remember that the disciples of Jesus were originally considered as followers of 'the Way'—and as such they held to a similar, yet distinct, set of beliefs. They focused on certain scriptural passages, like Isaiah 40, Jeremiah 31, and Habakkuk 2:4, but they drew different lessons from them.

The Jerusalem church

For years, the Prior of the Dormitian Abbey in Jerusalem Father Bargil Pixner has been setting out the argument for the identification of an Essene Quarter beside the traditional site of the Jerusalem church, where it is also believed that the Last Supper took place. He based his views upon the identification of 'the Essene Gate' in the German cemetery on Mount Zion. Josephus described the First Wall of Jerusalem (there were three walls) during the Roman siege of the holy city in *Jewish War* 5:144–5. Starting from the Hippicus Tower, the site of the citadel today, his description moved in an easterly direction to a place called Xystus before terminating at the western portico of the temple. From the same starting point, the description then moved in a westward and southerly direction along the wall, passed a place called 'Bethso' to the 'Gate of the Essenes'. Carrying on southwards pass the fountain of Siloam, the wall was followed eastwards and finally northwards to the eastern portico of the temple.

Beginning on the north at the tower called Hippicus, it extended to the Xystus, and then joining the council-chamber terminated at the western portico of the temple. Beginning at the same point in the other direction, westward, it descended past the place called Bethso to the gate of the Essenes then turned southwards above the fountain of Siloam; thence it again inclined to the east towards Solomon's pool, and after passing a spot which they call Ophlas, finally joined the eastern portico of the temple.

The gate was originally excavated by F. J. Bliss and A. C. Dickie in 1894–5 and re-excavated by Bargil Pixner, Doron Chen, and Shlomo Margalit between 1977 and 1988. This gate, made of well-cut stones, is 2.66 metres (or 9 feet) wide and what remain visible today are the slabs, a door socket, and drain. Pixner's argument that 'Bethso' was the latrine mentioned in the Temple Scroll is possible, although this Qumran scroll did not describe the real temple, but an idealized one. The ritual immersion pools nearby, called *miqvaot*, are similar to the ones found at Qumran and elsewhere.

Magen Broshi supported this identification of the Essene Gate and even suggested that the 1996 excavations of a nearby cemetery by B. Zissu would further bolster the theory. Apparently, the shaft graves of this cemetery are similar to the ones found at Qumran and are 'totally different' from the normal Second Temple burials'. But the graveyard is some 4.5 kilometres away (3.8 miles), southwest of the Essene Gate. Moreover, the Qumran burial practice is also evidenced at En El Ghuweir that is unrelated to Qumran based on the evidence of the ceramics. The Qumran burial practices are probably not unique nor even distinctive.

The name, 'the Essene Gate', may be further evidence of a quarter or perhaps a locality of Essenes. Other gates in Jerusalem were designated by the directions to which they led (e.g. Damascus Gate, Jaffa Gate, etc.), much like our motorway or highway sign-posts; however, this gate was named after a Jewish sect. It suggests that Essenes lived close to it, used it, and perhaps even built it. Both Philo and Josephus reported that Essenes lived in towns and villages of Palestine. Moreover, there was a certain Judas, during the time of Aristobulus I, who was an Essene and he used to teach his disciples in the court of the temple. It is likely that Essenes and/or urban sectarians lived there, but not the monastic type of sectarian.

Pixner and Rainer Riesner have contended that the New Testament has actually mentioned these Jerusalem Essenes in Acts 2:5–6, 'Now there were dwelling in Jerusalem Jews, devout men from every nation under heaven. And at this sound the multitude came together….' Moreover, in Acts 6:7, Luke, the author of this two-part work, even reported that 'a great many of the priests were obedient to the faith.' For Pixner and Riesner, the terms 'devout', 'multitude', and 'priests' in these verses were references to the Jerusalem Essenes.

Richard Bauckham, however, has offered a thorough critique of Pixner and Riesner's views. He argued that none of the textual evidence from Acts adduced to support a group of Jerusalem Essenes reflects Qumran terminology: the Greek word *hosios* ('holy') not *eulabes* ('devout') translates the Hebrew *hasid* ('piety', 'holy'); the Greek word *plethos* ('multitude') is not used in the same sense as the Qumran community's self-designation of *ha-rabbim*, the Hebrew for 'the many'. Moreover, the priests mentioned in Acts 6:7 could be any number of other priests and not necessarily Essenes.

As for the self-designations of the Jerusalem Church, Bauckham examined the terminology of 'the way', 'the holy ones/the saints', 'the church of God', and two terms purportedly to be equivalent to the *yahad*. On the first two, he concluded that there was no evidence of borrowing; the Qumran and Christian communities derived the terminology from common biblical sources, especially of Isaiah and Daniel 7. The Qumran scrolls' use of *qahal* ('assembly') or *edah* ('congregation') was more reflexive and did not have the sense that the Jeruslaem church invested into 'the church of God'. And finally, there is no equivalent to the Qumran *yahad* in the terminology of the Jerusalem church.

Pauline churches

Bauckham's views converge well with my own view on the relationship between the Qumran scrolls and early Christian churches. I believe that the various literary parallels between the Qumran scrolls and Pauline letters are best explained as the sharing of the same biblical sources and terminology, though with different understandings.

Take, for instance, the central concept of the new covenant previously discussed. Both the Qumran scrolls and Pauline letters drew on the same passage of Jeremiah 31:31–4 but infused it with meanings that cannot be easily reconciled. You will remember that the 'new covenant' signifies a renewing of the old covenant in the sectarian scrolls. By contrast, Paul's 'new covenant' is a new dispensation or stage in the unfolding of the divine will and is associated with the death and resurrection of Jesus ('this cup is the new covenant in my blood', 1 Corinthians 11:25).

It involves a new ethical and moral conduct, the following of 'the law of Christ', and a reinterpretation of Jewish scriptures (2 Corinthians 3).

When we place these two interpretations of Jeremiah 31 within the context of ancient Judaism, it becomes plain that the new covenant is sectarian in the sense that only members of sects focused on this concept. The whole of rabbinic literature ignores this concept; the only possible exception is *berit milah* or the covenant of circumcision, but its link to Jeremiah is tenuous at best. The model of a sectarian matrix explains why even though we find the same, key biblical passages quoted in the documents of different communities the lessons drawn from them are not the same.

It is likely that Essenes, if not also urban sectarians, came into contact with Christians in 1st-century Jerusalem. The Essene Gate was probably near a quarter or locality of Essenes living on what is known today as Mount Zion. But there is no conclusive evidence to prove that Jerusalem Essenes were mentioned in the New Testament. The early Jerusalem church may have used terms that were similar to those found in the Qumran scrolls, but upon closer scrutiny the words mean something else. It is suggested that a common sectarian matrix explains better the resemblance and disparity of the religious ideas and biblical quotations in the various documents. For instance, the Dead Sea Scrolls and Pauline letters often hit upon the same biblical text, but they do not understand it in the same way. The scrolls were not Christian scrolls and a comparison with the New Testament helped clarify their distinctiveness.

Chapter 12
The greatest manuscript discovery

The discovery of ancient manuscripts in caves near Khirbet Qumran has often been hailed as a momentous archaeological find and in the foregoing discussion I have given you an indication of just how the Dead Sea Scrolls have contributed to our understanding and knowledge of the Old Testament or the Hebrew Bible, Second Temple Judaism, and early Christianity. By way of conclusion, I would like to reflect briefly on their importance: are they really the greatest manuscript discovery of the 20th century? Do they warrant such a description?

It seems to me obvious that the claim of the 'greatest manuscript discovery' means one thing to the public and another to the scholar. The public expects by such a characterization something of an 'earth-shattering' significance that would overturn our received opinion of the origins of Christianity and Judaism; or at least a paradigm shift comparable in the sciences to the acceptance of the solar-centric view of the universe, the discovery of the laws of gravity, and the advances in quantum mechanics. This explains in part the sensationalization of the scrolls in relation to the person and work of Jesus and his early followers. Yet, claims of the kind have been unfounded or badly misguided and the expectations have been unfulfilled.

For the scholar, the description is much more specific; relative to what specialists of ancient Jewish history and biblical studies previously had in terms of evidence of the period the scrolls have been a boon, because they have contributed so much new information to a past that is only partially known. There are other finds of comparable significance for the ancient world and the Middle Ages.

To understand the scrolls' significance for scholarship, you have to realize that generally speaking the farther we go back in time, the less information we have. This may be difficult to comprehend in an age when information is readily available. We expect to find what we need to know about an airport, hotel, university, church, synagogue, cinema, or club at the click of the mouse or the tapping of a smart phone. Why should we get all excited about finding this or that dusty old scroll or fragment?

The Dead Sea Scrolls are important, first and foremost, for what they tell us about Second Temple Judaism and sectarianism. They allow us an insider's view of the thoughts and beliefs of one or more Jewish sects related to the Essenes and who were also comparable to early Christian groups. Their prime importance is historical, because there are no surviving Essenes today, even though some contemporary New Age groups do draw their inspiration from sectarian thought.

It has been argued that past scholarship has had a questionable tendency to describe the Jewish community of the scrolls in Christian terminology. Lawrence H. Schiffman contended that Qumran scholarship has been guilty of Christianizing the scrolls. Members of the community were not monks, led by a teacher of righteousness and bishop who performed baptisms, ate in a refectory, and copied manuscripts in a scriptorium—they were observant Jews, guided by a rabbi and teacher of righteousness, who performed ritual purifications in the *mikveh*, or ritual bath, ate communal meals, and copied texts in their library.

It is undeniable that by changing the terms of reference used in describing the Qumran community, Schiffman has dramatically altered our perception of the sectarians. He has stressed the continuity between the Qumran community and rabbinic Judaism, the form of Jewish religion defined by the rabbis after the destruction of the temple in 70 CE. For instance, he invoked the term *halakha*, or 'Jewish law', to describe discourse of a legal kind in the scrolls. But by doing so, he too can be challenged for interpreting the community anachronistically, since *halakha* properly belongs to rabbinic Judaism that postdates the Qumran scrolls. Is he not also guilty, in this case, of 'rabbinizing' the sectarians?

It seems to me that it hardly matters how we describe the Qumran community, so long as we know that we are merely drawing analogies for comparative purposes. The intention of any such comparison is to illuminate the less known with the better known. In this context, it is undeniable that the all-male community who followed a severe discipline of work and study as depicted in the Rule of the Community shows many traits that are similar to the Christian monastic movement. Asceticism, to name but the most obvious feature, is not a customary practice in Judaism but one that has a long and established tradition in Christianity.

The Dead Sea Scrolls are also important for Old Testament studies or Hebrew Bible scholarship in providing the earliest Hebrew and Aramaic manuscripts of almost all the biblical books. They have given us manuscripts that attest to the antiquity of the biblical texts, the reliability of the *textus receptus* of the Masoretic Text that underlies our English translations, and also an unexpected insight into the textual diversity before standardization. The scrolls illuminate the canonical process, the dual pattern of scripture and tradition, and the graded authority of compositions: biblical, non-biblical, and sectarian. Biblical scholarship is the primary beneficiary in this respect, but for some these findings have religious and theological implications on how to understand the Bible as the word of God.

Finally, the Dead Sea Scrolls are important for our understanding of the early churches and the New Testament. They underscore the historically and theologically vital point that Christianity began as a Jewish sect by providing us with the religious beliefs and practices of one or more contemporary groups. They serve as a foil that brings out the common biblical heritage, the shared sectarian matrix, and the distinctiveness of the Christian teachings.

There is no doubt that the Dead Sea Scrolls are the greatest manuscript discovery of the 20th century for Jewish studies of the Second Temple period and biblical studies. They have also become a cultural icon symbolizing anything that is ancient and important, and there is no better corroboration of this than the fact that you have just read this book, or at least turned to its final page!

References

Chapter 1: The Dead Sea Scrolls as cultural icon

Geza Vermes, Timothy H. Lim, and Robert Gordon, 'Oxford Forum for Qumran Research Seminar on the Rule of War from Cave 4 (4Q285)' *Journal of Jewish Studies*, 43 (1) (1992): 85–94.

Timothy H. Lim, *The Dead Sea Scrolls Electronic Reference Library*, vol. 1 (Oxford/Leiden: Oxford University Press and Brill Academic Publishers, 1997).

Wojciech Kowalski, 'Legal aspects of the recent history of the Qumran scrolls: access, ownership title and copyright' in *On Scrolls, Artefacts and Intellectual Property*, ed. Timothy H. Lim, Hector L. MacQueen, and Calum Carmichael (Sheffield: Sheffield Academic Press, 2001), p. 147.

Judith Anne Brown, *John Marco Allegro: Maverick of the Dead Sea Scrolls* (Grand Rapids: Eerdmans, 2005), pp. 157–8.

John Strugnell, 'The original team of editors', and Geza Vermes, 'Access to the Dead Sea Scrolls: fifty years of personal experience' in *On Scrolls, Artefacts and Intellectual Property*, ed. Timothy H. Lim, Hector L. MacQueen, and Calum Carmichael (Sheffield: Sheffield Academic Press, 2001), pp. 178–98.

The judgment and appeal decision of *Qimron v. Shanks* can be read in *On Scrolls, Artefacts and Intellectual Property*, ed. Timothy H. Lim, Hector L. MacQueen, and Calum Carmichael (Sheffield: Sheffield Academic Press, 2001), pp. 26–72 and 232–58; and in my article, 'Intellectual property and the Dead Sea Scrolls' *Dead Sea Discoveries*, 9 (2) (2002): 187–98.

Nimmer's work is entitled 'Copyright in the Dead Sea Scrolls: authorship and originality', and MacQueen's is 'Copyright law and the Dead Sea Scrolls: a British perspective', both in *On Scrolls, Artefacts and Intellectual Property*, ed. Timothy H. Lim, Hector L. MacQueen, and Calum Carmichael (Sheffield: Sheffield Academic Press, 2001), pp. 99–115.

Hector L. MacQueen, 'The scrolls and the legal definition of authorship' in *The Oxford Handbook of the Dead Sea Scrolls*, ed. Timothy H. Lim and John J. Collins (Oxford: Oxford University Press, 2010), pp. 723–48.

Chapter 2: The archaeological site and caves

The standard account of the Bedouin story is told by John C. Trever, who happened to have been spending 1948 in Jerusalem as Fellow at the American Schools of Oriental Research, in *The Dead Sea Scrolls: A Personal Account*, revised edn (Piscataway, NJ: Gorgias Press, 2003). More recently, see Weston W. Fields, *The Dead Sea Scrolls. A Short History* (Leiden: Brill, 2006); and John J. Collins, *The Dead Sea Scrolls. A Biography* (Princeton: Princeton University Press, 2013).

Charles Clermont-Ganneau, *Archaeological Researches in Palestine during the Years 1873-1874*, vol. 2 (London, 1896), p. 14.

Roland de Vaux, *Archaeology and the Dead Sea Scrolls* (Oxford: Oxford University Press, 1973).

Jodi Magness, *The Archaeology of Qumran and the Dead Sea Scrolls* (Grand Rapids: Eerdmans, 2002), pp. 63–9.

The survey was published in Hanan Eshel, Magen Broshi, Richard Freund, and Brian Schulz, 'New data on the cemetery east of Khirbet Qumran' *Dead Sea Discoveries*, 9 (2) (2002): 135–65.

Dennis Mizzi and Jodi Magness, 'Was Qumran abandoned at the end of the first century BCE?' *Journal of Biblical Literature*, 135 (2) (2016): 301–20. The revision of the periods of occupation is based on a reconsideration of the conflagration layer, the yellow sediment, and the three silver hoards.

Rachel Hachlili, 'The Qumran cemetery reassessed' in *The Oxford Handbook of the Dead Sea Scrolls*, ed. Timothy H. Lim and John J. Collins (Oxford: Oxford University Press, 2010), pp. 46–78.

Chapter 3: On scrolls and fragments

Stephen Reed, 'What is a fragment?' *Journal of Jewish Studies*, 45 (1994): 121–5.

Roland de Vaux, *Archaeology and the Dead Sea Scrolls* (Oxford: Oxford University Press, 1973), pp. 95–7.

Frank M. Cross, 'The development of the Jewish scripts' in *The Bible and the Ancient Near East*, ed. G. E. Wright (New York: Doubleday, 1961), pp. 144–202.

Chapter 4: New light on the Hebrew Bible

Frank M. Cross, 'The history of the biblical text in the light of the discoveries of the Judaean desert' *Harvard Theological Review*, 57 (1964): 281–99; and 'The Ammonite oppression of the tribes of Gad and Reuben: missing verses from 1 Samuel 11 found in 4QSamuel[a]' in *History, Historiography and Interpretation*, ed. H. Tadmor and M. Weinfeld (Jerusalem: Magness Press, 1983), pp. 148–58.

Ronald S. Hendel, 'Assessing the text-critical theories of the Hebrew Bible after Qumran' in *The Oxford Handbook of the Dead Sea Scrolls*, ed. Timothy H. Lim and John J. Collins (Oxford: Oxford University Press, 2010), pp. 281–302.

Emanuel Tov, *Textual Criticism of the Hebrew Bible*, 2nd edn (Assen: Royal Van Gorcum, 2001), pp. 114–17, 160–3.

James R. Davila, 'The name of God at Moriah: an unpublished fragment from 4QGenExod[a]' *Journal of Biblical Literature*, 11 (4) (1991): 577–82.

Timothy H. Lim, *Pesharim* (London: Continuum, 2002), ch. 4; *Holy Scripture in the Qumran Commentaries and Pauline Letters* (Oxford: Clarendon Press, 1997), pp. 143–6.

The translation for the extract from Kant is from Claus Westermann, *Genesis 12–36. A Commentary* (Minneapolis: Augsburg Publishing House, 1985), p. 354.

Chapter 5: The canon, authoritative scriptures, and the scrolls

Timothy H. Lim, *The Formation of the Jewish Canon* (New Haven, CT: Yale University Press, 2013); 'Authoritative Scriptures and the Dead Sea Scrolls' in *The Oxford Handbook of the Dead Sea Scrolls*, ed. Timothy H. Lim and John J. Collins (Oxford: Oxford University Press, 2010), pp. 303–22; 'A theory of the majority canon' *Expository Times*, 124 (7) (2012): 1–9; and 'An indicative definition of the canon' in *When Texts are Canonized*, ed. Timothy H. Lim (Atlanta: Society of Biblical Literature, 2017).

Chapter 6: Who owned the scrolls?

Dennis Mizzi, 'Qumran Period I reconsidered: an evaluation of several competing theories' *Dead Sea Discoveries*, 22 (2015): 1–42.

See the summary of Essene teachings in Geza Vermes and Martin Goodman, *The Essenes According to the Classical Sources* (Sheffield: Sheffield Academic Press, 1989), pp. 2–6. The translation of Pliny is from p. 33, and translations of Josephus are from pp. 43–4.

Roland de Vaux, *Archaeology and the Dead Sea Scrolls* (Oxford: Oxford University Press, 1973), pp. 103, 133–8.

Yizhar Hirschfeld, *Qumran in Context: Reassessing the Archaeological Evidence* (Peabody: Hendrickson, 2004), pp. 230–40.

Menachem Stern, *Greek and Latin Authors on Jews and Judaism*, vol. 1 (Jerusalem: The Israel Academy of Sciences and Humanities, 1976), p. 481.

Magen Broshi, 'Qumran: archaeology' in *Encyclopedia of the Dead Sea Scrolls*, ed. Lawrence H. Schiffman and James VanderKam, vol. 2 (Oxford: Oxford University Press, 2000), pp. 738–9.

An up-to-date critical review of the archaeology of Khirbet Qumran is found in Eric Meyers, 'Khirbet Qumran and its environs' in *The Oxford Handbook of the Dead Sea Scrolls*, ed. Timothy H. Lim and John J. Collins (Oxford: Oxford University Press, 2010), pp. 21–45.

John J. Collins, 'Foreword' in *Qumran, the Site of the Dead Sea Scrolls*, ed. Katharina Galor, Jean-Baptiste Humbert, and Jurgen Zangenberg (Leiden: Brill, 2006), p. vii.

Chapter 7: Literary compositions of the scrolls collections

Katharine Greenleaf Pedley, 'The library at Qumran' *Revue de Qumrân*, 5 (1959): 21–41.

Timothy H. Lim and John J. Collins, 'Introduction: current issues in Dead Sea Scrolls research' in *The Oxford Handbook of the Dead Sea Scrolls*, ed. Timothy H. Lim and John J. Collins (Oxford: Oxford University Press, 2010), pp. 1–18.

Sidney White Crawford and Cecilia Wassen, *The Dead Sea Scrolls at Qumran and the Concept of a Library* (Leiden: Brill, 2015).

J. A. Fitzmyer, *The Genesis Apocryphon of Qumran Cave I: A Commentary*, revised edn (Rome: Biblica et Orientalia, 1971); and Daniel Machiela, *The Dead Sea Genesis Apocryphon* (Leiden: Brill, 2012).

Daniel J. Harrington, *Wisdom Texts from Qumran* (London: Routledge, 1996), ch. 3.

Chapter 8: Jewish sectarianism in the Second Temple period

Martin D. Goodman, *The Ruling Class of Judaea: The Origins of the Jewish Revolt Against Rome AD 66–70* (Cambridge: Cambridge University Press, 1997).

Shaye J. D. Cohen, *From the Maccabees to the Mishnah*, 3rd edn (Philadelphia: Westminster Press, 2014), p. 124.

E. P. Sanders, *Paul and Palestinian Judaism* (Philadelphia: Fortress Press, 1977), pp. 425–6.

Hartmut Stegemann, 'Die Entstehung der Qumrangemeinde' (Bonn dissertation, 1971).

Lawrence H. Schiffman, *Reclaiming the Dead Sea Scrolls* (London: Doubleday, 1994).

Joseph Baumgarten, 'The disqualification of priests in 4Q fragments of the "Damascus Document", a specimen of the recovery of pre-Rabbinic Halakha' in *The Madrid Qumran Congress*, ed. J. Trebolle-Barrera and L. Vegas Montaner, vol. 2 (Leiden: Brill, 1992), pp. 503–4.

Chapter 9: The communities of the Dead Sea Scrolls

Roland de Vaux, *Archaeology and the Dead Sea Scrolls* (Oxford: Oxford University Press, 1973), pp. 109, 115, 117, 137–8.

Geza Vermes, *The Dead Sea Scrolls: Qumran in Perspective*, 2nd edn (London: SCM Press, 1994), ch. 4; Frank Moore Cross, *The Ancient Library of Qumran*, 3rd edn (Sheffield: Sheffield Academic Press, 1995); and J. T. Milik, *Ten Years of Discovery in the Wilderness of Judaea* (London: SCM Press, 1959). The two competing views of the recensional history of S are Sarianna Metso, *The Textual Development of the Qumran Community Rule* (Leiden: Brill Academic Publishers, 1997); and Philip Alexander, 'The redaction history of the *Serekh ha-Yahad:* a proposal' *Revue de Qumrân*, 17 (1996): 437–56.

Philip Alexander and Geza Vermes, *Qumran Cave 4*, vol. XIX: *Serekh Ha-Yahad and Two Related Texts;* vol. XXXVI: *Discoveries in the Judaean Desert* (Oxford: Clarendon Press, 1998).

John J. Collins, *Beyond the Qumran Community: The Sectarian Movement of the Dead Sea Scrolls* (Grand Rapids: Eerdmans, 2010); and 'Sectarian communities in the Dead Sea Scrolls' in *The Oxford Handbook of the Dead Sea Scrolls*, ed. Timothy H. Lim and John J. Collins (Oxford: Oxford University Press, 2010), pp. 151–72.

Elisha Qimron and James Charlesworth, *Rule of the Community and Related Documents* (Tübingen: J. C. B. Mohr/Paul Siebeck, 1994), p. 33 and notes 185 and 186.

Joseph Baumgarten, 'The Cave 4 versions of the Qumran penal code' *Journal of Jewish Studies*, 43 (2) (1992): 274.

The chronological hypotheses of Anti Laato and Emile Puech are discussed in Annette Steudel, '*acharit ha-yamim* in the Texts from Qumran' *Revue de Qumrân*, 16 (1993): 225–46.

John J. Collins, 'Essenes' in *The Anchor Bible Dictionary*, vol. 2 (London: Doubleday, 1992), p. 623; and 'The origins of the Qumran community: a review of the evidence' in *To Touch the Text: Biblical and Related Studies in Honor of Joseph A. Fitzmyer* (New York: Crossroad, 1989), p. 162.

P. R. Davies, *Sects and Scrolls: Essays on Qumran and Related Topics* (Atlanta: Scholars Press, 1996), chs. 11 and 12.

Charlotte Hempel, *Qumran Rule Texts in Context* (Tübingen: Mohr Siebeck, 2013).

Timothy H. Lim, *Pesharim* (London: Continuum, 2002), p. 76 and ch. 5.

Florentino Garcia-Martinez, 'Qumran origins and early history: a Groningen hypothesis' *Folia Orientalia*, 25 (1988): 113–36.

Chapter 10: The religious beliefs of the sectarian communities

E. Urbach, *The Sages: Their Concepts and Beliefs* (Cambridge, MA: Harvard University Press, 1987), p. 4.

Shemaryahu Talmon, 'The community of the Renewed Covenant' in *The Community of the Renewed Covenant*, ed. E. Ulrich and J. VanderKam (Paris: Notre Dame Press, 1994), pp. 3–24.

Mladen Popović, 'Physiognomic knowledge in Qumran and Babylonia: form, interdisciplinarity and secrecy' *Dead Sea Discoveries*, 13 (2) (2006): 150–76.

John J. Collins and Robert Kugler (eds), *The Religion in the Dead Sea Scrolls* (Grand Rapids: Eerdmans, 2000).

Chapter 11: The scrolls and early Christianity

Barbara Thiering, *Jesus the Man* (London: Doubleday, 1992).

Carsten Peter Thiede, *The Earliest Gospel Manuscript? The Qumran Fragment 7Q5 and its Significance for New Testament Studies* (Carlisle: Paternoster Press, 1992), p. 29.

R. H. Eisenman and Michael Wise, *The Dead Sea Scrolls Uncovered* (Shaftesbury: Element, 1992), pp. 24–33.

Geza Vermes, *The Complete Dead Sea Scrolls in English*, revised edn (London: Penguin Books, 2004), p. 189.

Geza Vermes, Timothy H. Lim, and Robert Gordon, 'Oxford Forum for Qumran Research Seminar on the rule of war from Cave 4 (4Q285)' *Journal of Jewish Studies*, 43 (1) (1992): 85–94.

Bargil Pixner, 'An Essene quarter on Mount Zion?' in *Studia hierosolymitana in onore del P. Bellarmino Bagatti.* Vol. 1: *Studi Archeologici*, ed. G. Bottini (Jerusalem: Franciscan Printing Press, 1976), pp. 245–84.

Magen Broshi, 'Essene Gate' in *Encyclopedia of the Dead Sea Scrolls*, ed. Lawrence H. Schiffman and James VanderKam, vol. 1 (Oxford: Oxford University Press, 2000), pp. 261.

Otto Betz and Rainer Riesner, *Jesus, Qumran and the Vatican* (London: SCM Press, 1994), ch. 10.

Richard Bauckham, 'The early Jerusalem Church, Qumran and the Essenes' in *The Dead Sea Scrolls as Background to Postbiblical Judaism and Early Christianity,* ed. J. R. Davila (Leiden: Brill Academic Publishers, 2003), pp. 66–89.

Timothy H. Lim, 'Qumran scholarship and the study of the Old Testament in the New Testament' *Journal for the Study of the New Testament*, 38 (1) (2015): 68–80; and 'Studying the Qumran Scrolls and Paul in their historical context' in *The Dead Sea Scrolls as Background to Postbiblical Judaism and Early Christianity,* ed. J. R. Davila (Leiden: Brill Academic Publishers, 2003), pp. 135–56.

Joseph A. Fitzmyer, *The Dead Sea Scrolls and Christian Origins* (Grand Rapids: Eerdmans, 2000); and George J. Brooke, *The Dead Sea Scrolls and the New Testament* (London: SPCK, 2005).

Chapter 12: The greatest manuscript discovery

Jean Duhaime, *Les Esséniens de Qumrân. Des Esotéristes?* (Paris: Editions Fides, 1990).
Lawrence H. Schiffman, *Reclaiming the Dead Sea Scrolls* (London: Doubleday, 1994), p. 18.

Further reading

English translations

Martin Abegg, Jr, Peter Flint, and Eugene Ulrich, *The Dead Sea Scrolls Bible* (New York: HarperCollins, 1999). English rendering of all the Qumran biblical scrolls.

Geza Vermes, *The Complete Dead Sea Scrolls in English*, revised edn (London: Penguin, 2004). This is the standard English translation of the non-biblical scrolls.

General introductions

John J. Collins, *The Dead Sea Scrolls. A Biography* (Princeton: Princeton University Press, 2013).

Philip R. Davies, George J. Brooke, and Phillip Callaway, *The Complete World of the Dead Sea Scrolls* (London: Thames and Hudson, 2002). An attractive book, full of illustrations.

Peter W. Flint, *The Dead Sea Scrolls* (Nashville: Abingdon, 2013).

Lawrence H. Schiffman, *Reclaiming the Dead Sea Scrolls* (Philadelphia: Jewish Publication Society, 1994). Argues that the scrolls should be reclaimed for Judaism.

James VanderKam, *The Dead Sea Scrolls Today* (Grand Rapids: Eerdmans, 1994). An accessible and balanced introduction.

Geza Vermes, *The Dead Sea Scrolls: Qumran in Perspective*, 2nd edn (London: SCM Press, 1994). A classic introduction.

Commentaries and companions

The scrolls are not easily accessible to the uninitiated. Readers interested in pursuing various topics more fully should begin by reading the scrolls in Vermes's translation, which also provides short introductions to each text. There are a few commentary series, notably *The Oxford Commentary on the Dead Sea Scrolls* (<http://www.ocdss.div.ed.ac.uk>) and the Eerdmans Commentaries on the Dead Sea Scrolls. Other useful resources include the following.

John J. Collins, *Apocalypticism in the Dead Sea Scrolls* (London: Routledge, 1997). An authoritative discussion of the religious world view of the scrolls.

Michael A. Knibb, *The Qumran Community* (Cambridge: Cambridge University Press, 1987). A balanced and reliable commentary on some of the most important scrolls.

Timothy H. Lim et al., *The Dead Sea Scrolls in Their Historical Context* (London: T&T Clark, 2000). Useful articles that contextualize the scrolls within Second Temple Judaism.

Timothy H. Lim, *Pesharim* (London: Continuum, 2002). An advanced introduction to the sectarian commentaries.

Timothy H. Lim and John J. Collins, *The Oxford Handbook of the Dead Sea Scrolls* (Oxford: Oxford University Press, 2010). The standard, up-to-date critical review of areas of scrolls research.

Lawrence H. Schiffman and James C. VanderKam, *Encyclopedia of the Dead Sea Scrolls*, 2 vols (Oxford: Oxford University Press, 2000). A useful work of reference.

Scrolls and the Hebrew Bible

Timothy H. Lim, *The Formation of the Jewish Canon* (New Haven: Yale University Press, 2013); and 'A theory of the Majority Canon' *Expository Times*, 124 (7) (2012): 1–9. Proposes a new theory for the formation of the Jewish canon based on the evidence of the scrolls.

Emanuel Tov, *Textual Criticism of the Hebrew Bible*, 2nd edn (Assen: Royal Van Gorcum, 2001). A technical reference for Old Testament textual criticism.

Eugene Ulrich, *The Dead Sea Scrolls and the Origins of the Bible* (Grand Rapids: Eerdmans, 1999). A collection of important articles on the Qumran biblical scrolls.

Scrolls and sectarianism

Albert Baumgarten, *The Flourishing of Jewish Sects: An Interpretation* (Leiden: Brill, 1997). Attempts to explain why there were so many Jewish sects during this period.

Shaye J. D. Cohen, *From the Maccabees to the Mishnah*, 3rd edn (Philadelphia: Westminster Press, 2014). Standard textbook of early Judaism.

Jutta Jokiranta, 'Sociological approaches to Qumran sectarianism' in Timothy H. Lim and John J. Collins (eds), *The Oxford Handbook of the Dead Sea Scrolls* (Oxford: Oxford University Press, 2010), pp. 200–31. Discusses latest sociological studies in relation to the study of the scrolls.

Scrolls and the early Church

Otto Betz and Rainer Riesner, *Jesus, Qumran and the Vatican* (London: SCM Press, 1994). Informative articles on the connection between the scrolls and Christianity.

George J. Brooke, *The Dead Sea Scrolls and the New Testament* (London: SPCK, 2005). Collection of articles on biblical interpretation.

Timothy H. Lim, 'Qumran scholarship and the study of the Old Testament in the New Testament' *Journal for the Study of the New Testament*, 38 (1) (2015): 68–80.

Appendix: hitherto unknown texts

The discovery of the scrolls brought to light hundreds of texts that were never preserved for posterity. These texts may be categorized by various literary genres. I will draw your attention only to the most important ones. Readers who are interested in reading all the non-biblical scrolls can look them up in the various anthologies that have been published; *The Complete Dead Sea Scrolls in English* by Geza Vermes is the standard English translation.

Sectarian texts

The words 'sect' and 'sectarianism' in English carry with them negative connotations of heterodox teachings, religious marginalization, political disaffection, and fanaticism. Most of these undertones are inapplicable to sects that flourished in the period between 200 BCE and 100 CE. Sects functioned more like schools of thought and practice; they had disciplinary rules and procedures of initiation; they had their distinctive teachings, but also shared common beliefs and practices with the majority of people from whom they have separated.

Scholars believe that numerous texts among the scrolls represent the Qumran community of the Essenes. This view relies upon the triple linking of the Khirbet Qumran site with the scrolls found in the caves and the sect of the Essenes. Without prejudicing the discussion, it may be noted that several of the scrolls are related to each other in depicting one or more communities, Essene or otherwise, that are sectarian. These scrolls are identified as sectarian by what they say about the respective community, the world view (often described as 'eschatological perspective'), the self-belief that they are the true Israel, and the terminology that they use, such as *parash*, 'to separate'; *yahad*, 'community'; *ha-rabbim*, 'the many'; *pesher*, or 'interpretation'; *moreh ha-tsedeq*, 'the teacher of righteousness'; *ha-cohen ha-rasha*, 'the wicked priest'; *mattiph ha-cazab*, 'the liar'; and *kittim*, or 'Kittim' (identified with the Romans).

Several texts are called rules or *serakhim* (singular: *serekh*). They are orders and regulations of communal life or prescriptions for the order of battle in the eschatological war. The Damascus Document is one such rule.

In 1910, two texts entitled *Fragments of a Zadokite Work* were published by Solomon Schechter as part of a massive collection of fragments (220,000) of medieval Hebrew and Jewish writings found in the Ben Ezra Synagogue in Old (Fustat) Cairo, Egypt. These writings were found in a *genizah*, or storeroom for worn-out books. This work, now known as the Damascus Document, is a text that describes the origins and laws of a group of pious Jews who separated from the majority who are considered transgressors of the laws. In all, there are ten copies of this document found in Caves 4–6, and they attest to a connection between the scrolls and the Karaites, a Jewish sect that refused to accept the authority of the rabbis.

The Rule of the Community *(serekh ha-yahad*, or 1QS) describes the organization, practices, beliefs, and origins of a community that saw itself as the sons of light. It is extant in numerous copies found in Caves 1, 4, and 5. Appended to it are two other rules, the Rule of the Congregation, which presents the community at the end of days, and the Rule of Blessings, which is a compilation of liturgical texts.

There are several other 'rules' that govern specific aspects of the community, such as the initiation process, the disqualification of priests for inappropriate behaviour, the ceremony of renewing the covenant, the purities that are to be maintained, and observance of Jewish law. Rules of a different kind, namely the War Scroll (or *milhamah*) and other texts, relate the military strategy for a cosmic battle at the end-time between the sons of light and the sons of darkness.

Biblical interpretation

A group of some twenty-five scrolls interpret larger and smaller passages from the Hebrew Bible using the technical term *pesher*. The Hebrew word *pesher* simply means 'interpretation', but the exegetical procedures and hermeneutical perspectives are distinctive. There are two types of *pesharim* (plural of *pesher*), the continuous and thematic. The continuous *pesharim* are running commentaries on the verses and phrases of a biblical book by the use of a regular pattern of biblical quotation, introductory formula, and comment. They comment on Isaiah, several of the psalms and seven of the twelve Minor Prophets. The most important of these *pesharim* is the Habakkuk Pesher (1QpHab, where p = *pesher*). The thematic *pesharim*, on the other hand, organize their commentary around a theme, such as the person and work of the heavenly redeemer figure, Melchizedek (11QMelch). The pesherite technique can also appear in isolated exegesis of individual verses (e.g. CD (Cairo Damascus Document) 4:14). The *pesharim* interpret the biblical texts as predictions that have been fulfilled in their time; they contemporize or actualize scriptural prophecies.

Hymn

The Hodayot, or Thanksgiving Psalms, from Cave 1 is a long scroll of eighteen columns in which an individual speaker and community gives thanks to the Lord. There are six other copies of the same text from Cave 4. The hymns found in this scroll can be divided between those that are 'hymns of the teacher' and the 'hymns of the community'. The speaker, who suffers persecution and asks God for salvation, has been identified by scholars as the teacher of righteousness, a key figure in the Damascus Document and the *pesharim*. The 'hymns of the community' express the beliefs and hopes of a group of pious members who look forward to the deliverance of the just at the end of days. Although the language of the Hodayot is allusive, drawn especially from the Psalms, it does contain verbal affinities to the *pesharim*. Its connection to the other sectarian scrolls is also established by the presence of a thanksgiving hymn at the end of the Community Rule. It also quoted a previously unknown wisdom text called '4Qinstruction', or *musar le-mevin*.

Law

The 4QMMT (= *miqsat ma'aseh ha-torah*; or 'some precepts of the torah') scroll, was previously mentioned in connection with copyright and intellectual property. It is a three-part text that includes a calendar, a list of laws, and an admonition. At its centre is a discussion of twenty or so legal issues (e.g. the impurity of a stream of liquid) that distinguish the various parties, known only as 'we', 'you' (singular and plural), and 'they'. The editors, Elisha Qimron and John Strugnell, believe that this text recounts the early history, if not prehistory, of the Qumran Essene community, before it separated from the majority of the people.

Calendar and priestly courses

There are numerous texts among the scrolls that follow a 364-day, solar calendar. There are texts that apply this solar calendar to the dating of the flood story in Genesis (4Q252) and the division of the priests for their duty at the temple (4QMishmarot, or 'priestly courses'). There are also texts that synchronize the solar calendar and the priestly courses with the waxing and waning of the moon as required by the lunar calendar. The lunar cycle that counts 354 days in a year was the official calendar of the temple. The 364-day solar calendar as such is not sectarian, since it is also found in 1 Enoch and Jubilees. Its application to the dating of the flood story in Genesis, however, qualifies it as sectarian.

Various literary texts

Finally, there are numerous other texts that can be categorized by previously known literary genres, including apocalypses, apocrypha, physiognomies (texts that examine the physical features of a person as indicative of his spiritual life), wisdom texts, prayers, blessings, and testaments. The sectarian character of these texts is debated.

Index

Pope Benedict XVI *see* Ratzinger, Joseph

SOCIAL MEDIA
Very Short Introduction

Join our community

www.oup.com/vsi

- Join us online at the official Very Short Introductions **Facebook** page.
- Access the thoughts and musings of our authors with our online **blog**.
- Sign up for our monthly **e-newsletter** to receive information on all new titles publishing that month.
- Browse the full range of Very Short Introductions online.
- Read **extracts** from the Introductions for free.
- If you are a teacher or lecturer you can order inspection copies quickly and simply via our website.